CHRISTMAS 2013

NICOLE - A GOOD BOOK
FOR A GOOD CAUSE - HOPE
YOU ENJOY IT!
LOVE, DAN

W9-AZE-494

Recipes to the Rescue

Stray Rescue
of Saint Louis

Recipes to the Rescue

A Community Cookbook

Stray Rescue of St. Louis
2320 Pine St.
St. Louis, MO 63103

314.771.6121

Mission and History of Stray Rescue of St. Louis

I am often asked how I started Stray Rescue of St. Louis. I ask myself that, too. I never devised a game plan or had a vision; I guess it was born out of necessity. I hated my job as a flight attendant. I figured there had to be more to life than saying, "chicken or beef." Little did I know that this career move would one day evolve into two no-kill shelters with a legion of over 400 volunteers and 300 foster families, and have an impact on the stray dog crisis in America. I love the dogs I save. I feel their pain, so I keep up the act of "Dog Man" or, as a homeless man calls me, "Coyote Man," so those canines don't suffer and die. That's pretty much why I became the founder of Stray Rescue.

I suffer from social anxiety. I have some phobias. I am gay. I am a shy, private kind of guy—by no means a hero. I have been thrust into the dog limelight from a previous book about my work. It forces me to try to be more outgoing and confident. You know, exude that Rambo-type of confidence.

In 1990 I learned the fine art of cutting dog hair. It's not something I really wanted to do, but I thought it would at least point me in the direction of my dream of working with animals. I'd see stray dogs—some in packs—pass by the Lafayette Square grooming shop where I worked. In an effort to get them off the streets, I'd make the normal calls to the local shelters and government agencies, only to find out that these dogs simply are out of luck. I started to think of ways to catch them, and before long I invented some wacky capture methods. I also enlisted friends to help save these poor guys. Each year, this makeshift organization grew as I overloaded everyone I knew with a stray dog.

Stray Rescue officially was born in 1998 as a full-fledged non-profit organization and shelter. I still have no idea how I did it, except that I had no choice. Stray Rescue has received numerous accolades from the American Red Cross and also has received national media attention from Animal Planet, National Geographic, the Weather Channel and Forbes Magazine. Now with Quentin on board, his story has been featured in People Magazine and on It's a Miracle television show. In the National Geographic feature, Mary Ann Mott wrote: "In St. Louis, Randy Grim, founder of Stray Rescue, is out on the streets every day feeding 50 or more mutts. If these wild dogs don't die of sheer starvation, he said, diseases such as parvovirus, heartworm, or intestinal parasites usually kill them. Their average life span is one to two years. Many of the animals he sees were once "bait dogs"—smaller, passive animals used to train fighting dogs. Great Dane puppies are commonly used, he said, and wire is twisted around their legs to hold them down, so they can't run while being mauled during training sessions. "If they live, they are just discarded onto the streets," said Grim. The animals are recognizable by their missing limbs, and scars from the brutal attacks. Since starting in 1991, I am credited with saving 5,000 feral dogs, all of which—through months of gentle, loving care—have been turned into house pets and adopted by new families. Some have even gone on to become therapy animals, bringing joy to people in hospitals and nursing homes." Animal Planet's "Wild Rescues" television show featured Stray Rescue in action, saving dogs and cats from abuse and neglect from a dilapidated abandoned puppy mill in Cuba, MO. More than 17 lives were saved, but the woman responsible never was prosecuted. Since 1998, more than 45 households have participated in the Stray Rescue foster family network. These generous people take in sickly, traumatized animals and, with time and the support of professional animal trainers and behaviorists, give back healthy, loving companions ready for adoption. Stray Rescue's foster network is the largest and most effective program of its kind in the St. Louis area. Stray Rescue has made a significant impact and become a voice for stray animals everywhere. With fabulous volunteers, veterinarians, trainers, behaviorists, shelters and programs, I continue to be amazed at how this organization has evolved. But there is so much more work to do because these poor animals continue to suffer. Some days it feels as if I'm fighting a never-ending battle, but it's a battle that I must wage—for their sake.

Stray Rescue's mission is to lead the way towards making St. Louis a compassionate city where every companion animal knows health, comfort, and affection, and no stray is euthanized merely because he or she has been abandoned, abused, or neglected. As part of our mission, Stray Rescue is out on the streets daily taking a progressive, proactive approach to establishing a permanent resolution to the stray companion animal problem through dedicated rescue efforts, sheltering, community outreach programs, education, collaborations, and the encouragement of responsible pet guardianship.

Virtually all of the pets we save have been abused and neglected. They've been dumped on highways, or remote country roads. Abandoned in public parks, empty houses and dark alleys. We've even saved dogs left chained behind buildings after their owners had moved away.

Rescued animals often make the best pets. Pets from Stray Rescue seem to understand that they have a second lease on life. In return for a little affection and attention, these remarkable animals reward their new owners with a love and loyalty unmatched anywhere.

Randy Grim

Annual Events

- *SPRING FOR STRAYS* at Harry's Restaurant and Bar

- *URBAN WANDERERS* is an art exhibit sponsored by Stray Rescue of St. Louis and SLUMA, showcasing homeless companion animals and bringing awareness to the problem of stray animals. The theme of this year's exhibit is "The Plight of the Street Dog," which focuses on the hardships of strays and the uplifting stories of their rescues and recoveries.

- Please join us for our most important and most special fundraising event of the year. Our *HOPE FOR THE HOLIDAY'S GALA* brings together a year of compassionate companion animal rescue and the generosity of the giving season. Check the website for information regarding this year's event.

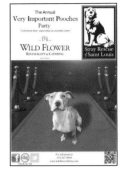

- *ANNUAL GOLF TOURNAMENT*

- *VERY IMPORTANT POOCHES PARTY* at Wildflower Restaurant

Ways to Help

SAVING PETS & ENRICHING LIVES: Stray Rescue of St. Louis helps save abandoned pets from disease, neglect and death on the streets. Make a donation to Stray Rescue at any Dierbergs checkout! Just tell your cashier the amount you wish to donate. You will receive a receipt with the amount donated for your records. 100% of your donation goes directly to Stray Rescue.

ORDER STRAY RESCUE MERCHANDISE from the comfort of your own home! Shop the Online Store at www.Strayrescue.org. Your purchase has a direct impact on providing care for our beloved homeless companion animals—thank you for your support!

BENEFIT WINES AND OTHER SHOPPING PARTNERS: For more information check out the "Shopping Links" under the "How to Help" tab on www.strayrescue.org website.

BRICK BY BRICK, BUILDING A SHELTER ONE BRICK AT A TIME: All the proceeds from these memorial bricks go towards the construction of our main adoption and dog apartment area; a space that will be incredibly enriching and comfortable for the dogs. And believe it or not, we care about people too! We want them to know the joy a shelter dog can bring. With this area completed, it will be easier than ever to find the perfect companion, leading to more adoptions and highlighting the human-dog bond. This phase of shelter renovations will consist of replacing existing temporary kennels with 20 extraordinary dog apartments, as well as a laundry room, kitchen, and shelter manager's office.

BARRET'S BUDDIES: Barret's Buddies is Blues defenseman Barret Jackman's program to help neglected and abused animals from Stray Rescue of St. Louis.

THE STRACKS FUND: Donate via our website to support our emergency medical care fund. Many of the dogs that are rescued have life threatening medical issues and often need emergency care. The Stracks fund is dedicated to help pay for the needed veterinary care.

OUR WISHLIST: If you would like to help us in our efforts to save homeless animals, the following is a list of items we use most often. Stray Rescue of St. Louis depends on the generous donations received by the public. We thank you from the bottom of our hearts!

- Purina ONE adult dry dog food
- Pop-Top Canned Dog Food
- Blankets and Towels (gently used)
- Braunschweiger, Cheese Whiz, Peanut Butter, and Hot Dogs
- Martingale/No Slip dog collars (Medium & Large Size)
- Cat & Dog Beds
- Cat & Dog Collars
- Cat & Dog Leashes
- Cat Toys
- Kong Toys
- Nylabones
- Large Wire Crates (36"–52")
- Cat & Dog Treats
- Dog Harnesses (Medium & Large Size)
- Litter and Litter Boxes
- Garbage Bags (55 Gallon and 13 Gallon)
- Cleaning Supplies
- OdoBan, Lysol, or other Air Sanitizers
- Dye-Free Laundry Detergent
- Liquid Fabric Softener
- Bleach
- Paper Towels
- Toilet Paper
- Surgical Gloves
- Volunteers
- Financial Donations

Stray Rescue Programs

Stray Rescue of St. Louis was officially born in 1998 but in just a few short years has grown to offer 15 different programs in support of our goals. Listed below is a brief description of each program that will give you an idea of the breadth of our operations.

RESCUE AND REHABILITATION PROGRAM: This is our main operation involving the rescues of homeless dogs (and some cats) who live on the city streets. Many dogs are abandoned or dumped by their guardians and others are born on the street and are feral. Depending upon the degree to which dogs are feral, many must be humanely trapped. As a no-kill shelter, these dogs are medically rehabilitated, spayed/neutered and adopted into loving homes. It is critical to rescue these homeless animals in order to end the overpopulation problem. Most people do not realize that one male and one female dog can produce 67,000 dogs in just seven years according to Spay Day USA. In addition to saving dogs, we are preventing hundreds of thousands of puppies from being born on the street and contributing to the overpopulation crisis.

ANIMAL REGULATION CENTER (ARC) ASSIST PROGRAM: Stray Rescue takes in as many injured dogs and pregnant female dogs from the ARC as possible. In 2004 Stray Rescue provided the funding that allowed the city pound to migrate from using the gas chamber to lethal injection for euthanization. These dogs are medically rehabilitated and placed into loving homes.

TRIAL ADOPTION PERIOD (TAP): This program gives people who are interested in adopting a dog the opportunity to take the dog home for the weekend and see if the Stray Rescue dog gets along with other dog and/or cat family members. It also allows people the opportunity to take a dog home for the weekend (certain conditions apply) so that our dogs get a chance to learn how to live in a home and get out of the shelter for a few days.

RUNNING BUDDIES: This is a fun, unique, and meaningful way to stay in shape while enriching the lives of shelter dogs as they await their loving forever homes. The Stray Rescue Running Buddies program ensures these dogs get plenty of exercise, attention, and exposure to environments outside of the shelter. Perfect for everyone, from those who are easing into their newfound workout routine to seasoned marathon runners looking to liven up their training, motivation to get fit is never a problem when you know your walking/jogging pooch partner is waiting.

PANDA PROGRAM: Stray Rescue's Panda Program is a hospice program for dogs. In this program you agree to take a dog into your home who has a limited amount of time left to live. The dogs in this program have been diagnosed with terminal illness or may be very old or both. They are deserving of a home where they can live out their remaining life with love and dignity and not have to die alone. Quality of life is the most important part for us all, and together we can give these dogs a happy, safe, and loving end of life.

STRAY RESCUE HIKING CLUB: This enrichment club aims to improve the lives of shelter dogs through hiking. In addition to providing these dogs with much needed time out of the shelter it gives anyone who loves to hike, backpack or trail run the opportunity to meet their perfect four legged companion. For more information go to www.fourdirectionshiking.com.

SENIORS FOR SENIORS PROGRAM: Senior citizens preferably on a fixed income but not limited to, who adopt an older dog are able to do so without paying the adoption fee, and, if necessary, Stray Rescue will provide food and medical care for the life of the dog. In addition, a person who adopts a senior dog which has a chronic health problem may be eligible for complimentary veterinarian support for the ongoing medical condition for their dog. This program has been funded by Mrs. Arthur Lieber.

POST ADOPTION PROGRAM: This program provides behavioral training for dogs in which their adoption potential is limited due to a behavioral issue or for a guardian who adopted a Stray Rescue dog who is experiencing difficulties adjusting to their new home. This program is designed to make sure every dog finds their perfect home and is able to stay with their new family.

COMMUNITY COLLABORATIONS: Stray Rescue often partners with other animal welfare organizations to either to raise money or provide mutual support for various programs. In addition, Stray Rescue has helped other animal welfare organizations by taking in dogs, providing medical care or other assistance as needed. A few of our collaborations are noted below: "Loosen the Leash" This program was created by Cindy Vickers who is a dog behaviorist/trainer and who wanted to help at risk teenagers experience the unconditional love of a dog. She, along with the help from the St. Louis Support dog organization, Stray Rescue and the St. Louis City juvenile detention centers—this program was initiated to give at risk teens a chance to learn how to train a dog and experience the value of the human-animal bond for their own lives. "Nooterville" We open our shelter and provide the volunteers who pass out vouchers for low cost spay/neuter surgery for eligible residents. "Metro Animal": We provide financial assistance to this organization which specializes in the trapping of feral cats and providing spay/neuter surgeries.

SHELTER/RESCUE OUTREACH: Randy Grim and Stray Rescue provides assistance to other animal shelters and rescue groups who are working to end the use of the gas chamber in their local or county animal shelters. Randy has traveled to North Carolina, Oklahoma, Georgia and New Mexico to share his experience and advice with local officials so they can improve the welfare of the animals in their jurisdiction. Many shelters converted to lethal injection which is a more humane method of euthanization as a result of Randy's efforts. He also works with shelters and rescue groups wanting to increase adoptions or migrate towards a no-kill philosophy. In addition, Randy mentors groups interested in learning how to trap feral dogs and rehabilitating them so they become adoptable.

ABANDONED, NOT FORGOTTEN: Stray Rescue has formed a hotline number for any banker, real estate agent, police officer or fireman to call when they find a dog or cat that has been left behind in a home for any reason such as foreclosure. Stray Rescue has partnered with Joe Richardson and Whitehouse Kennels to help house these animals until they are adopted.

FAMILIES WITH PAWS: The purpose of this to share information and free pet care resources, one zip code at a time. Through this program we offer spays and neuters, rabies and distemper shots as well as microchips. All of these services are available for both dogs and cats. Call 314-771-6121 extension 259.

SHELTER IN PLACE (SIP) PROGRAM: This program provides medical/health care to the pets of low-income families and individuals who have shown a commitment to keeping their companion(s) but do not have the financial means to do so. Each participating household is assigned a caseworker who will coordinate spay/neutering of the pet through Stray Rescue's veterinary facility. Stray Rescue also provides food and supplies. However, the value of the program extends well beyond medical benefits and general care. Caseworkers provide education on proper pet care, which encourages responsibility, fosters self-reliance, and results in the empowerment of the family to be a part of the solution, as well as advocates for companion animals.

POP (PICK ONE & PUSH): This offers businesses, schools, and community groups an incredibly rewarding way to make a huge difference in the lives of shelter animals by finding them loving forever homes. Each group is assigned a specific adoptable Stray Rescue dog or cat with the singular goal of finding a forever home for that animal. Not only will you make a difference by ensuring a four-legged friend a life filled with comfort, warmth, and love, but the program also encourages teamwork, advocacy, and communication.

TEACHING LOVE AND COMPASSION (TLC): We have a small volunteer committee dedicated to providing a few select educational programs for school children and community groups. Topics include pet guardianship and the importance of spaying and neutering our pets.

Volunteer Opportunities

At Stray Rescue, we're always looking for dedicated volunteers! We couldn't survive without them. To volunteer, fill out our on-line volunteer form, or call us at 314-771-6121. Your help is greatly appreciated! Some of the events and activities that we can always use help for are as follows:

- People to care for and walk animals staying at our two shelters in St. Louis City, even if it is one hour a week or everyday.
- People to help lead adoption events, or handle shelter at adoption events.
- Recruitment of committed volunteers and fosters.
- People to work with fundraising and fundraising events.
- Help with information booths and merchandise tables at special events.
- Volunteers for Stray Rescue events (Urban Wanderers, Holiday Gala, Golf Tournament, block parties, etc)
- Group Volunteering:
- If you can help with any of these events, or have other talents that you think we would find helpful, please give us a call or fill out our on-line volunteer application. Thank you!

In order to best accommodate large groups from schools, businesses, and other organizations, please contact us to schedule an orientation. We are delighted to have you as volunteers, but depending on the size of your group, we may need to set up a personal orientation time.

Becoming a Stray Rescue foster parent is one of the most helpful, heartfelt things you could possibly do for a homeless companion animal. As a foster, you provide a temporary loving home for an abandoned dog or cat until he or she finds a forever home. Many of those we rescue have lived difficult lives on harsh city streets, and fosters are essential to showing these animals what it means to trust, feel safe, and experience comfort. Whether your foster is with you for several days or several months, the knowledge that you helped immensely will last a lifetime

STRAY RESCUE REHABILITATION ENRICHMENT PROGRAM (REP): This program has been designed for volunteers that seek to take extra steps in the rehabilitation process of a particular dog. We are aware that certain bonds form between individuals and select dogs, and that these relationships are highly valuable to the dogs during their time within our shelter. By participating in the REP, you are committing to the mental and physical wellbeing of this animal all the way up until the point of adoption.

Stray Rescue of St. Louis
2320 Pine St.
St Louis, MO 63103
314.771.6121
www.strayrescue.org

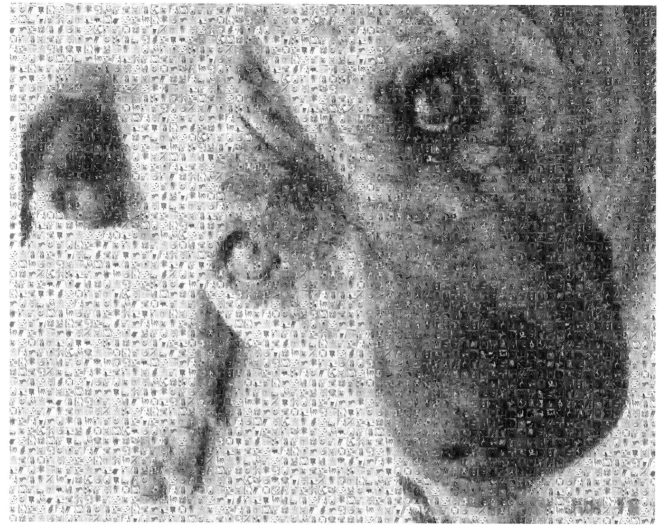

Photo of Carrot Top, collage composed of the many rescued dogs passing through Stray Rescue doors.

This cookbook is dedicated to all the current, past, and future Stray Rescue Dogs. Special thanks go to Randy Grim, Jenn Foster, all the staff and hundreds of volunteers that work tirelessly to provide safety, care, training, and love until they find their forever homes. Stray Rescue of St. Louis has been instrumental in educating people on animal abuse. Most importantly, it has been responsible for the formation of the Mayor Francis Slay Animal Abuse Taskforce and working with law enforcement and the court system to prosecute those responsible for abuse. I am so proud to be part of this organization.

I want to recognize Brooklyn based artist, Dean Russo, for donating the art for the cover of the cookbook. I asked and he responded with a resounding YES! Dean strives to promote all dogs in a positive light and supports many rescue organizations. Thank you for your contribution. I am grateful to all the contributors and advertisers who sponsored the project. With your support, we were able to fund the initial printing. Special recognition goes to 90 Degrees West in Lafayette Square who supported the book when it was little more than an idea.

Thank you to all the dedicated volunteers who shared the photos that can be seen throughout the cookbook. In addition, I could not have completed this cookbook without a small group of volunteers who helped sell advertising or contributed personally. Stray Rescue of St. Louis has the most dedicated volunteers I have ever had the privilege to work with. I am lucky to call many of you friends. I don't

have room to list you all individually, but you know who you are. Special thanks to volunteer Tom Morrison who contributed his special photographs pictured on the back cover of the book.

Lastly, thank you to the St. Louis community that contributed recipes. This book would not be possible without the many contributions of delicious recipes. Special thanks to our local chefs and personalities who showed so much enthusiasm for the project and never hesitated to contribute. We are lucky to live in a town that cares so much for animals.

Thank you to our book designer Cathy Wood, and editors Scarlett Stoppa and Donna Biffar. I appreciate their enthusiasm for this project and all the professional guidance they provided. Ron Elz was instrumental in providing his expertise in publishing and connecting us to our printer, Taylor Publishing.

Lastly, but certainly not least, I want to thank my husband Brian Deneau. You have been an extraordinary support from start to finish. You have helped me with ideas and I could not have done it without you.

This cookbook has been a labor of love. Our family began volunteering over two years ago and Stray Rescue of St. Louis has quickly became my passion. I hope you all love it as much I loved working on it. Bon Appetit! Sarah Deneau

TaBLe of Contents

Ducati

DEDICATED TO
Randy Grim, staff and volunteers of Stray Rescue St. Louis

Cover artwork donated by Dean Russo Art
http://www.deanrussoart.bigcartel.com

First Edition 2013
Released in conjunction with Mound City Publishing
Published by Stray Rescue St. Louis
2320 Pine St., St Louis, MO 63103
314.771.6121
314.781.0001

© Copyright 2013 Stray Rescue of St. Louis

ISBN-13:978-0-615-85385-7

Book designed by Cathy Wood
Email: woodce@swbell.net

Printed in the United States of America

All rights reserved. This book may not be reproduced, in whole or in part, in any form (beyond that copying permitted by Section 107 and 108 of the U. S. Copyright Law and by reviewers or reporters for the public press), without written permission from the copyright holder.

St. Louis Notables

Orion

APPETIZERS AND BEVERAGES

Winslow's Home Rolled Omelet

CARY MCDOWELL
Executive Chef, Winslow's Home

12 large pastured, cage-free eggs
1 C whole milk
¼ C unbleached, all-purpose flour
Salt and pepper to taste
1 bag baby spinach, preferably organic
1 (4 oz) can good-quality roasted, peeled preserved peppers
3 oz fontina cheese, shredded

Preheat oven to 350°F. Grease lightly a half-pan cookie sheet and line with a piece of parchment paper. Ensure that the paper rises above the edges all around so that you may pour liquid inside without it leaking. Mix the eggs, milk, salt, pepper, and flour. Make sure there are no lumps, and pour into the prepared pan. Gently mix in some of the peppers, and disperse them evenly. Add of the raw spinach on top of the liquid mix (this will bake in). Carefully place the pan into the preheated oven and bake until eggs "set up" throughout. This usually takes 8-10 minutes. When set, remove from oven, top with remaining ingredients and all of the cheese. Return to oven for 2 more minutes. Remove, let stand no more than 5 minutes (just long enough to cool so you can roll). Carefully roll, using the excess paper as a tool, snugly–like a jellyroll. Let stand at least 10 minutes so that the roll may "set up." Remove paper and slice; serve with small tuft of mixed salad greens and/or breakfast potatoes.

Creamy Garlic Shrimp

RICK SANBORN
Morning Host, KHITS 96.3

2 Tbsp butter
1 lb shrimp, peeled and deveined
¼ C chopped onion
1 Tbsp capers, sliced to release flavor
1 Tbsp minced garlic
Juice of 1 lemon
5 Tbsp Philadelphia Cooking Crème® savory garlic

Preheat oven to 350°F. Melt 2 Tbsp butter in 7-inch baking bowl. Add 1 lb of peeled and deveined shrimp (wild-caught recommended). Top with ¼ C chopped onion, 1 Tbsp of capers, and 1 Tbsp of minced garlic. Squeeze lemon over all. Add 5 Tbsp of Philadelphia Cooking Crème savory garlic and spread on top of other ingredients in the baking bowl. Cover bowl with aluminum foil and bake 20 minutes. Remove aluminum foil and change oven from bake to broil. Broil uncovered on upper shelf for 5 minutes. Remove from oven and let stand 2 minutes. Enjoy!

Spicy White Castle Dip

GUY FAVAZZA "FAVAZZ"
KSHE 95 Real Rock Radio

10 White Castle® hamburgers
1 (8 oz) package cream cheese
3 packets White Castle mustard
½ C onion, finely chopped
9 oz chunked hot Pepper Jack cheese
⅔ C milk
2 Tbsp parsley flakes

Mix cream cheese and mustard together and spread on bottom of large, shallow microwave-safe serving dish; spread onions evenly on top. Place burgers in food processor until blended and spread over onions. Slice cheese into chunks, add milk, and melt in microwave for 1-2 minutes. Stir until creamy. Pour cheese mixture over burgers. Sprinkle parsley flakes on top. Heat for 3-4 minutes in microwave, or bake in conventional oven for 20 minutes. Serve with a large bag of tortilla chips. Serves a crowd. 🌀

Farmer's Cheeezzzy Spicy Guacamole Bean Dip

SHERRY FARMER
Oldies 103.3 KLOU

1 (16 oz) can Old El Paso® spicy, fat-free refried beans
3 large avocados
3 Tbsp fresh lime juice
2 (8 oz) containers light sour cream
1 packet Old El Paso® hot and spicy taco seasoning mix
1 (10 oz) can Rotel® original, diced tomatoes and green chilies, drained
2 C shredded sharp cheddar cheese
Tortilla chips

Preheat oven to 350°F. Spread a layer of spicy fat-free refried beans in the bottom of an 8x8 quart glass baking dish. Pit and peel the avocados and place in a bowl. Mash avocados together with lime juice and spread on top of the refried beans. In a separate bowl, stir together the sour cream and the taco seasoning mix. Spread over the avocado. Drain diced tomatoes and green chilies, and place over the sour cream layer. Follow up with a layer of shredded cheese. Heat the dip for 15-30 minutes or until heated through and the cheese is a bit melted. Serve warm with tortilla chips. Serves 8. 🌀

Janet Conners' Southern Caviar (aka Pimento Cheese)

JANET AND LARRY CONNERS
News Anchor

5 roasted red bell peppers, diced
32 oz white cheddar cheese, grated in two sizes
1 C finely chopped green olives
½ C olive oil mayonnaise
1 Tbsp parsley flakes
½ tsp ground black pepper
Dash of cayenne
1 C shredded yellow cheddar cheese

Preheat oven to 500°F. Combine all ingredients and stir.

Directions (To Roast Red Peppers):
Lightly rub whole bell peppers with olive oil and bake at 500°F for 25-30 minutes, turning once or twice. Remove from oven and place them in a bowl. Cover with plastic wrap for 15-20 minutes. This helps the skin come off very easily. Remove skin, stems, and seeds. Do not rinse the seeds! You'll lose some of the flavor. Dice red peppers. You can buy jars of roasted red peppers–even some that are already diced, but roasting the peppers yourself is easy, much less expensive, and the difference in taste is worth the extra effort.

This recipe is modified from two Charleston, South Carolina recipes. We enjoy our Southern Caviar on Triscuits® (black pepper and olive oil flavor) and on celery. It's also delicious added to grilled steaks before serving. Makes great sandwiches, especially added to the cheeses for a grilled cheese sandwich. ◎

Shrimp and Mango Ceviche

COREEN SAVITSKI
Show Me St. Louis

¾ lb (about 30) medium shrimp, peeled and deveined
½ C finely chopped red onion
6 Tbsp lime juice
¼ C cilantro, roughly chopped
1 large mango, peeled, pitted and chopped
1 tomato, cored and chopped
1-2 jalapeño peppers, seeded, if desired, and finely chopped
¾ tsp fine sea salt

Bring a medium pot of generously salted water to a boil. Add shrimp and cook until pink and cooked through, 1-2 minutes. Drain, rinse under cold running water, and drain again. Chop shrimp into ½-inch pieces and transfer to a large bowl. Add onion, lime juice, cilantro, mango, tomato, jalapeño, and salt. Toss well. Cover and chill until cold, about 60 minutes. Serves 6-8. ◎

Cheesy Herb Cashew Spread

CARYN DUGAN
Stlveggirl.com

1½ C raw cashews, soaked for 60 minutes
2 tsp unfiltered apple cider vinegar
2 Tbsp tomato paste
1 Tbsp dried oregano
½ tsp each onion powder, savory, marjoram, and cloves
2 Tbsp nutritional yeast flakes

Process cashews, vinegar and tomato paste. Once creamy, add the rest of the ingredients. Chill for at least 30 minutes. Use as a spread, dip, or condiment!

Chef Pam's Crab Slaw Martini

PAM SMITH
Your Home Bistro

½ C olive oil
3 Tbsp lemon juice
3 Tbsp white wine vinegar
1 tsp Dijon mustard
2 dashes Tabasco sauce
1 Tbsp fresh snipped chives + extra for garnish
1 clove garlic, minced
1 tsp sugar
¼ tsp Old Bay® seasoning
¼ tsp salt
White pepper to taste
3 broccoli stalks, shredded
1 large carrot, shredded
1 C radicchio, shredded
2 C Napa cabbage, shredded
¼ C red onion, small julienne
1 lb king crab,*removed from shell and shredded
½ lemon, sliced for garnish
*weight includes shell

In a small bowl, blend the lemon juice, white wine vinegar, Dijon mustard, Tabasco, chives, garlic, sugar, Old Bay seasonings, salt, and white pepper. Slowly whisk in the olive oil to make the dressing. In a large bowl, combine the broccoli, carrots, radicchio, Napa cabbage, and red onion. Blend as much dressing as needed into the vegetables to make the slaw. Divide the slaw between six chilled martini glasses. Place a portion of crab on top of the slaw in each glass. Sprinkle chives over crab and garnish each glass with a wedge of lemon. Serves 6.

Dried Beef Sandwiches

CHRIS HAYES
Investigative Reporter, Fox 2 KTVI

1 (8 oz) package cream cheese
½ C sliced green onions
5 oz jar dried beef
8-12 thin slices cucumber
4 bagels*
*other sliced bread will work, such as the thin bread from Pepperidge Farms®

Assemble layers starting with cream cheese, then green onions, and then dried beef. Keep the cucumber separate until it is time to eat, or place the slices between beef to keep the bread from becoming soggy. Serves 4.

My Mom invented this during a car trip to Palo Duro Canyon. ⊚

North African Style Hummus

BEN LESTER
Executive Chef, Mosaic Modern Fusion Restaurant

CLAUS SCHMITZ
Chef/Owner, Mosaic Modern Fusion Restaurant

2 (15 oz) cans garbanzo beans
6 lemons, juiced
3 Tbsp tahini
3 cloves garlic
½ C olive oil
¼ C filtered water
Pita chips or grilled pita bread

Blend garbanzos in food processor with lemon, water, and garlic until very smooth. Add a few ice cubes while blending if puree gets too warm. Once everything is smooth, add the tahini and slowly add the olive oil with machine running. Add salt to taste. Top with choice of olives, feta cheese, lemon, olive oil, pita chips, or grilled pita bread. ⊚

Ahi Tuna Tartare

BEN LESTER
Executive Chef, Mosaic Modern Fusion Restaurant

CLAUS SCHMITZ
Chef/Owner, Mosaic Modern Fusion Restaurant

2 lbs #1 grade tuna, diced
½ C sesame oil
1 C soybean oil
½ C rice wine vinegar
½ C honey
1 ginger coin, crushed
1 bunch cilantro, chopped
1 oz diced shallot
1 oz minced garlic

Mix all ingredients in a large bowl. Salt and pepper to taste. Serve with wonton crisps. ◎

Mike Roberts' Speedy Brat and Cheese Dip

MIKE ROBERTS
Meteorologist, KSDK News Channel 5

16 oz Velveeta® cheese
1 (16 oz) jar Pace® picante sauce
5-6 bratwursts
1 package of hot dog buns

Preheat the backyard grill. Place cheese and desired amount of picante sauce in a microwave-safe bowl or crock-pot. Melt cheese and picante sauce together. Microwave brats for 1 minute to ensure the inside is done. Don't do more than two at a time. Finish grilling the brats on the grill for 6-9 minutes. When done, cut one up and drop it into the cheese mix. Place the other on a bun. Bam! You're ready to eat and hit the road! Serves 4.

Are you a storm chaser always on the go? If you simply don't have the time to get a full meal together before running out the door to catch up with a tornado, or, a few kids and a dog who've left the house looking like it was hit by one—maybe you need to try this! ◎

Pigs Under a Blanket

JUSTIN HAIFLEY
Executive Chef, The Tavern

2½ lbs pork butt, cut into 1-inch cubes
4½ tsp salt
3 tsp black pepper
3 tsp chili powder
6 tsp paprika
1½ tsp cayenne
3 tsp cumin
1 tsp coriander
6 cloves roasted garlic
1½ tsp fresh oregano, minced
½ bunch cilantro, minced
2 Tbsp sugar
1½ Tbsp tequila
1½ Tbsp red wine vinegar

Toss ingredients in a large bowl until herbs and spices are evenly combined. Chill ingredients on a sheet tray in the freezer until about half frozen. Grind ingredients through a grinder attached with a ¼-inch-sized die. Form into 1-inch-sized balls. Cut out 1½-inch squares from a sheet of puff pastry. Cover balls with puff pastry and brush with egg wash. Bake at 350°F for 12-15 minutes until puff pastry is golden brown and chorizo is cooked through. Serve with Beer Cheese Sauce (recipe below). 🌀

Beer Cheese Sauce

JUSTIN HAIFLEY
Executive Chef, The Tavern

1 C onion, diced
1 tsp minced garlic
2 Tbsp butter
2 Tbsp flour
12 oz Sophie® beer
1 C heavy cream
1 tsp Sriracha sauce
1 Tbsp salt
6 slices American cheese
4 C shredded cheddar cheese

Sauté onions and garlic in butter until translucent. Add flour and cook while stirring for 2 minutes. Add beer and whisk until incorporated. Add cream and heat until cream starts to boil. Add cheese, Sriracha, and salt. Cook until cheese is melted. Blend sauce in a blender until smooth and strain through a fine mesh sieve. 🌀

Mail Order Bride

MIKKI JONES
Bistro 1130

2 oz house cucumber and lavender-infused vodka
¾ oz fresh-squeezed lime juice
3-6 mint leaves
2 oz ginger beer (Goslings® recommended)

In a pint glass, add the first 3 ingredients. Add ice to a cocktail shaker, shake and strain over new ice in a copper mug or your favorite Collins glass. Top with ginger beer, and garnish with a lively mint sprig.

Cucumber-Lavender Vodka

Pour one liter of your favorite vodka into a large container. Peel and chop one whole cucumber, add to vodka. Chop one whole cucumber with peel on, add to the vodka. Measure 2 oz dried or fresh lavender. Add to the vodka. Leave the vodka covered with plastic wrap at room temperature overnight. Transfer to the refrigerator and let infuse 2-3 days more. Strain through a fine mesh strainer and store in the refrigerator. Keeps up to 2 months. ◎

Popcorn Stuff

PAUL COOK
Y98

6 C popped popcorn
2 C Cheerios® cereal
1 C Crispix® cereal
2 C pecans
½ C margarine
¼ C corn syrup
1 C brown sugar
½ tsp baking soda
1 tsp vanilla

Combine popcorn, Cheerios, Crispix, and pecans in large bowl. Cook without stirring the margarine, corn syrup, and brown sugar. Bring to a boil and remove from heat. Add baking soda and vanilla. Mix. Pour over cereal combination and bake in large pan for 60 minutes at 250°F, stirring every 15 minutes. Then party! ◎

Awesome Nachos

LAURA NOWLIN
Author, "If He Had Been With Me."

6 green onions, sliced, white parts and tops separated
3 Tbsp oil
1 whole chicken breast, cooked and shredded
1 C salsa or pico de gallo
½ (12 oz) package of tortilla chips
1 (8 oz) package shredded cheddar/Monterey Jack cheese blend
1 large tomato, diced
2 cloves crushed garlic

Preheat oven to 350°F. In a 12-inch skillet over medium heat, cook and stir the garlic and white parts of the green onions in canola oil until tender. Mix in shredded chicken, salt, and pepper. Toss until well coated with oil. Stir in salsa. Arrange tortilla chips on a large baking sheet. Spoon the chicken mixture over tortilla chips. Top with cheddar/Monterey Jack blend and tomato. Bake 10 minutes, or until cheese has melted. Remove from heat and sprinkle with green onion tops before serving. ◎

Spinach Ball Appetizers

KELLY STABLES
Actress, TV Land's "The Exes"

2 packages chopped frozen spinach, thawed and squeezed until no water left
2 C Pepperidge Farm® stuffing
1 large onion, chopped fine or use onion soup mix
4 eggs
½ C Parmesan cheese
¾ C melted butter
1 minced garlic or garlic salt
½ tsp thyme
Salt and pepper to taste

Mix and chill 2 hours. Shape into small balls. Freeze. Thaw when ready to use. Place on a cookie sheet. Bake 30 minutes at 300°F.

This recipe originally came from my 91 year old grandma. ◎

Cheese Deluxe Appetizers

KELLY STABLES
Actress, TV Land's "The Exes"

1 loaf Pepperidge Farm® white bread, very thinly sliced
2 jars Kraft Old English® cheese spread
½ C margarine, softened
Dash Tabasco sauce (optional)
½ tsp onion powder
½ tsp beau monde seasoning
¾ tsp dill weed
¼ tsp Worcestershire sauce
Dash cayenne pepper

Remove crusts from bread. Mix all remaining ingredients together. Spread each slice of bread with cheese mixture. Stack 3 slices high and spread top and sides with cheese mixture. Cut into 4 squares. Spread cheese mixture on remaining 2 sides. Repeat with remainder of bread slices. Freeze on cookie sheet, then place in plastic bag for later use. Bake at 350°F for 15 minutes or until toasted.

This recipe originally came from my 91 year old grandma.

Green Curry Mussels

ALAN MCREYNOLDS
Chef, West End Grill and Pub

1 lb fresh Prince Edward Island mussels, cleaned with beards removed
1 can unsweetened coconut milk
1 C white wine
1 Tbsp green curry paste
2 Tbsp minced garlic
2 Tbsp minced ginger
1 C minced cilantro
1 tsp minced jalapeño
1 tsp chili paste
1 Tbsp soy sauce
½ C minced red onion
3 Tbsp olive oil
1 Tbsp lime juice
Crostini for dipping

In large pot heat oil, then add onions, garlic, ginger, and jalapeño. Sauté until onions become translucent, 3-4 minutes. Add curry paste and toast with the aromatics a few minutes, being careful not to let burn. Add white wine, coconut milk, chili paste, soy sauce, lime juice, and cilantro. Bring to a boil. Add mussels and cover until mussels open, 3-5 minutes. Discard any unopened mussels. Serve on large platter with crostini, reserving any leftover broth for dipping.

Scape's Hot Chocolate with Homemade Marshmallows

ERIC KELLY
Executive Chef, Scape Bistro

Hot Chocolate

1 disk Ibarra® Mexican chocolate

3 C whole milk

Place chocolate disk into a saucepan with the milk. Over moderate heat, bring mixture to a simmer, whisking constantly. Once chocolate is melted, ladle into warmed mugs. Place a marshmallow on top. Adult version—add a splash of Godiva® caramel liqueur.

Marshmallows

2 oz gelatin powder

1½ C Karo® light corn syrup

1½ C water

½ tsp salt

4 C sugar

4 egg whites

6 oz water

1 Tbsp vanilla extract

Bloom gelatin in water. Set aside to bloom for 10 minutes. Place sugar, salt, corn syrup and 1½ C water in a saucepan over high heat. Cook sugar to 240°F, checking with a candy thermometer. Meanwhile, dice the bloomed gelatin and place into the bowl of an electric mixer fitted with a whip attachment. Once sugar is 240°F, remove from heat and pour over the gelatin while mixing on medium speed. Whip for 30 seconds. Add egg whites and vanilla. Whip on high speed until white and fluffy. Line a 13x18 cookie sheet with parchment paper. Dust very liberally with cornstarch to completely coat. Pour warm and fluffy marshmallow into the dusted pan. Using an offset spatula, spread marshmallow evenly. Dust the top surface very liberally with more cornstarch.

Black and Bleu Mussels

ERIC KELLY
Executive Chef, Scape Bistro

1 Tbsp olive oil
2 Tbsp bacon lardons
7 garlic cloves, roasted
1 lb Prince Edward Island mussels
1 oz white wine
2 oz chicken stock
3 oz butter, diced
2 Tbsp blue cheese
½ jalapeño, sliced thin

Wash mussels under cold running water, scrubbing away the beards. Heat oil in a hot skillet over moderate heat. Add the bacon and garlic, cook 1 minute until bacon is golden brown. Add mussels and cook one minute until mussels begin to open. Add wine and stock. Bring to boil and reduce by half. Add butter and swirl to emulsify with reduction. Pour into a warm service bowl, top with cheese and jalapeño. Serve with crusty bread. ◎

Pineapple Salsa

SEAN D. SCOTT
Chef, Square One Brewery

2 pineapples
1 red onion, finely, diced
1 jalapeño, minced
½ Tbsp chopped garlic
6 scallions, diced
Juice of 3 limes
1 bunch cilantro
6 Roma tomatoes, diced
Salt and pepper

Peel and quarter the pineapples. Remove the core from each piece and grill them on all sides. As the pineapple cools, dice the other vegetables and mix everything else together. Once the pineapple has cooled, cut the pieces in half length-ways and then dice fine. Mix together. ◎

SIDE DISHES

Cowboy Potatoes

JULIE TRISTAN
Host, Show Me St. Louis, KSDK-TV and Proud Stray Rescue Volunteer

2 lbs frozen hash browns
½ C chopped onions
1 can cream of chicken soup
10 oz cheddar cheese, shredded
8 oz sour cream
½ C melted margarine
Salt and pepper to taste
2 C crushed cornflakes

Preheat oven to 350°F. Combine all ingredients, except cornflakes, in a large bowl. Pour into a greased 9x13 casserole dish. Cover with the cornflakes and bake 45 minutes.

We have this at almost every family function! They are soooo good and I always take leftovers home! Sometimes I just eat THIS for dinner! Don't tell my hips! 🌀

Best Coleslaw Ever!

CINDY COLLINS
Oldies 103.3 KLOU

1 large head cabbage, shredded
2 medium carrots, shredded
1 tsp celery seed
1 C vegetable oil*
1 C white sugar
4 oz white vinegar
1 tsp salt
1 tsp ground mustard
1 medium onion, quartered
*do not use olive oil

Combine cabbage and carrots in a large bowl. In a blender, combine vegetable oil, vinegar, sugar, salt, ground mustard and onion. Blend until smooth. Pour over cabbage mixture and mix well. Add celery seed and toss lightly. Refrigerate for several hours, or overnight, for best flavor.

I serve this quite often and rarely have leftovers! The dressing turns a creamy white color, but it does not contain mayonnaise, so it is safe to sit on the counter during a party or potluck. 🌀

Couscous Risotto

CASSIE VIRES
Home Wine Kitchen

3 Tbsp olive oil
1 onion, diced
½ C shallots, chopped
4 C Israeli couscous
2 C white wine
2 C vegetable stock
1½ C butternut squash, shredded
1½ C Swiss chard, chopped
1 C heavy cream
1 C freshly grated Parmesan cheese
3 Tbsp unsalted butter
2 Tbsp Italian parsley, chopped

Heat the olive oil in a large pot over medium heat. Once the oil is hot, add the onion and shallots and sauté until soft, but not browned. Stir in the couscous and season with salt and pepper. Add the wine, scraping any browned bits from the bottom of the pot, and stir until all the wine has evaporated. Add the stock and simmer until the liquid is reduced by half. Gently fold in the squash and Swiss chard, then add the heavy cream. Cook over medium heat until creamy and thickened. Stir in the Parmesan, butter, and parsley and continue stirring until well-blended. Adjust seasoning and serve immediately. Garnish with additional Parmesan, if desired. Serves 8. 🌀

Parmesan Brussels Sprouts

CHERISE PATTERSON
Owner/Operator, 2 Girls 4 Wheels Food Truck

10 Brussels sprouts
2 Tbsp Parmesan
1 Tbsp olive oil or butter
Dash of salt and pepper
Squeeze of lemon

Chop sprouts into quarters. Sauté sprouts in butter or olive oil. Sprinkle with lemon, Parmesan, salt, and pepper. Sauté until Parmesan is brown. 🌀

Stacked Eggplant Parmesan

DIERBERGS SCHOOL OF COOKING

1 medium eggplant (about 1 lb)
¼ C flour
½ tsp California garlic pepper
½ C egg substitute
1 C whole-wheat or regular panko bread crumbs
3 Tbsp grated Parmesan cheese
Olive oil non-stick cooking spray
2 C marinara sauce, divided
1 (8 oz) ball fresh mozzarella cheese, cut into 6 thin slices
1½ tsp grated Parmesan cheese

Preheat oven to 400°F. Cut eggplant crosswise into 12 slices, each about ½-inch thick. On sheet of waxed paper, combine flour and garlic pepper. Place egg substitute in shallow dish. In second shallow dish, combine panko and the ¼ C Parmesan. Coat eggplant slices with flour mixture, dip into egg, then coat with panko mixture. Arrange in single layer on parchment-lined baking sheet; lightly coat each slice with cooking spray. Bake until tender, 20-24 minutes. Spread ¼ C of marinara sauce in bottom of 9x13 baking dish, coated with non-stick cooking spray. Place 6 of the eggplant slices in single layer over sauce. Top each slice with 1 slice mozzarella and 1 Tbsp marinara sauce. Add another layer of eggplant; top with remaining marinara sauce. Bake until sauce is bubbly and cheese begins to melt, about 8 minutes. Sprinkle ¼ tsp Parmesan over each eggplant stack. ◉

Couscous-Stuffed Peppers

DIERBERGS SCHOOL OF COOKING

4 red, yellow, or green bell peppers, halved lengthwise and seeded
½ lb lean ground beef
½ C chopped onion
1 (15 oz) can black beans, rinsed and drained
1 (14.5 oz) can petite, diced tomatoes
½ C water
1 tsp Italian herb seasoning
½ tsp Cajun/Creole seasoning
1 C whole-wheat or original couscous
1 C shredded mozzarella cheese

Preheat oven to 375°F. Place peppers cut-side up in 9x13 baking dish; pour ¼ C water into pan. Cover and bake until crisp-tender, about 20 minutes; drain well. Heat a large non-stick skillet over medium-high heat. Crumble ground beef into skillet. Add onion; cook stirring occasionally until onion wilts, 2-3 minutes. Drain off any fat. Stir in beans, tomatoes, ½ C water, and seasonings; bring to a boil. Remove from heat; stir in couscous. Cover and let stand 5 minutes. Fluff couscous mixture with fork; spoon into partially baked pepper halves. Cover tightly and bake, 25-30 minutes. Top peppers with cheese. Bake uncovered until cheese is melted, about 5 minutes. ◉

Beet Tart Tatin with Arugula Salad

JONATHAN DREJA
Executive Chef, Franco's Restaurant

2 medium-sized red beets
⅓ C sherry vinegar
½ C brown sugar
1 sprig rosemary, leaves only
½ tsp Dijon mustard
1 sheet puff pastry
8-10 garlic chips (recipe below)
2-3 slices black truffle peelings
10-12 roasted pistachios
1 Tbsp extra virgin olive oil
Salt and pepper to taste

Peel the beets and slice them into 1/16-inch rounds. Bring a pot of water to a boil and season lightly with salt and pepper, blanch the beets for 8 minutes or until al dente. Remove from water and let cool to room temperature. Combine the sherry vinegar, rosemary leaves, and brown sugar in a nonreactive pot and bring to a boil. Turn down to a simmer and let reduce until thickened to a corn syrup consistency. Remove the glaze from heat and stir in the Dijon mustard. While still hot, use ¾ of the glaze to evenly coat the bottom of a 9-inch sauté pan. Shingle the beet slices, starting from the outer edge of the pan working towards the center in concentric circles until the pan in full. Season the top with salt and pepper. Roll out a sheet of puff pastry to cover the pan and trim it so there's no overhang on the pan. Place the pan in a 400°F preheated oven and bake 18-20 minutes or until the pastry is golden brown and crispy. Let the tart Tatin cool for about 5 minutes, and place a plate wide enough to cover the pan over it and flip the Tatin out of the pan onto the plate. Drizzle the remaining glaze over the top and around the plate. Mix the arugula with the garlic chips, pistachios, black truffle peelings, and a quality extra virgin olive oil (such as OMED® Selection). Season with a little salt and pepper. Gently mound the salad on top of the tart tatin. Serves 4.

Garlic Chips
2 cloves garlic, thinly sliced
Olive oil

Place the garlic in a small pan and add enough olive oil to cover. Turn the stove on to medium heat and, stirring occasionally, allow the garlic to cook until golden brown. Remove from the oil and allow to dry on paper towels.

Smoked Salmon Chips

REX HALE
Chef, The Restaurants of the Cheshire Inn

Kettle potato chips
½ lb chipotle cream cheese
½ lb hot smoked salmon, flaked, or substitute store-bought hot smoked salmon
1 red onion, diced
2 oz capers
2 Tbsp dry spice seasoning

Dry Spice
2 C salt
1⅓ C sugar
⅔ C dry thyme
2 C New Mexico chile powder
⅔ C cayenne pepper
⅔ C garlic powder

Layer chips with smoked salmon, diced red onion, capers, and chipotle cream cheese (recipe below). Garnish with dry spice seasoning.

Chipotle Cream Cheese
2 Tbsp chipotle in adobe, canned
½ lb cream cheese, room temperature
¼ C chives, finely snipped
1 lime, juiced
½ Tbsp kosher salt
½ Tbsp sugar

Place chipotles in food processor and puree until smooth. Add cream cheese and mix well. Add remaining ingredients and mix until fully incorporated. Periodically scrape down so all ingredients mix together. Set aside. Chipotle cream cheese can be prepared up to two days in advanced chilled in a refrigerator. ◉

SOUPS AND SALADS

Seafood Gazpacho

LEISA ZIGMAN
KSDK News Channel 5

6 large ripe tomatoes, washed and coarsely chopped, saving the juice

1 red pepper, cored, seeded, and coarsely chopped

1 yellow pepper, cored, seeded, and coarsely chopped

2 jalapeño peppers, cored, seeded, and coarsely chopped

3 stalks celery, diced

2 red onions

2 shallots

2 cucumbers, peeled, seeded, and chopped

½ C red wine vinegar

½ C olive oil

½ C bread crumbs

1½ C V8® vegetable juice

¼ tsp cayenne pepper

½ C chopped fresh cilantro, salt and fresh ground pepper to taste

2-3 cans lump crab meat

3 avocados

Whisk vinegar, oil, tomato juice, and V8 together in a small bowl. Puree the vegetables in small batches, using a blender or food processor. Add tomato juice mixture and bread crumbs, as necessary. Do not puree completely; mixture should be chunky and crunchy. Stir in cayenne and cilantro and salt and pepper to taste. Cover and chill for at least 4 hours. Before serving, add lump crab meat and avocado. Serves 8-10.

Roasted Butternut Squash Soup

BEN LESTER
Executive Chef, Mosaic Modern Fusion Restaurant

CLAUS SCHMITZ
Chef/Owner, Mosaic Modern Fusion Restaurant

2 butternut squash, cut in half, seeded
1 vanilla bean, split and scrape out pulp
2 C spring water, filtered water
½ C heavy cream
2 oz butter
Agave nectar or sugar
Kosher salt

Roast butternut squash halves until soft, at 350°F on a sheet tray or pan coated with vegetable oil. When cool enough to handle, scoop out flesh and transfer to a small pot. Add water and vanilla bean pulp to pan. Bring to a simmer, then transfer to blender. Puree on high speed in batches if necessary. After 30 seconds, add the butter and keep blending until smooth, 2-3 minutes. Transfer puree to soup pot and hand whisk in the heavy cream, agave nectar to taste, and salt to taste. Water may need to be adjusted to obtain the correct consistency. ⊚

Chicken Tortilla Soup

KATIE FELTS
KSDK News Channel 5

1½ lbs chicken breast, cooked, save broth
4 C chicken broth
1 large can diced tomatoes
2 cans Rotel® diced tomatoes and green chilies
1 small red onion, chopped
2 garlic cloves, minced
½ tsp ground cumin
1 Tbsp ground red chili powder

Cook chicken until it shreds easily. Place everything in a soup pot and simmer for 15 minutes. If you choose, add juice of two limes before serving. Soup can be garnished with choice of tortilla chips, chopped green onions, fresh cilantro and shredded cheese right before serving. ⊚

Taco Soup

KATIE FELTS
KSDK News Channel 5

1 lb lean ground beef
1 large onion, chopped
1 (16 oz) can pinto beans
1 (15 oz) can kidney beans
1 (14.75 oz) can cream style corn
1 (15 oz) can hominy
1 (10 oz) can Rotel® tomatoes
1 envelope Hidden Valley Ranch® dressing mix
1 envelope taco seasoning

Brown ground beef and drain fat. Place into a large pot. Add other ingredients. Do not drain juices from cans. Mix together and bring to a boil. Simmer on low setting for 30 minutes or more. Serve with garnishes of sour cream, green onions, tortilla chips, and shredded cheese. ⊚

Italian Wedding Soup

FRANK CUSUMANO
Sportscaster, KSDK News Channel 5

½ lb ground veal
½ lb ground sirloin
1 large egg
1 C grated Romano cheese
½ C Italian bread crumbs
1½ C orzo
Salt and pepper
2 Tbsp finely chopped fresh Italian parsley
8 C chicken broth
1 small head escarole, washed, trimmed, and chopped
½ C grated Parmesan or Romano cheese

Heat the broth in a large pot. Add orzo. Mix together the meats, cheese, egg, bread crumbs, parsley, salt, and pepper. Once the broth is hot, reduce it to a simmer. Form small meatballs, about 1-inch in diameter, and drop them into the broth. Cook for about 5 minutes and then drop in the escarole. Cook for a few more minutes or until all meatballs float to the top and the escarole is wilted. Skim off any foam that develops as the meatballs cook. Serve in individual soup bowls, with a good helping of grated cheese on top. Buon Appetito! Serves 8. ⊚

Gwen's Favorite White Chili

SANDY MILLER
News Anchor, Fox 2

2 Tbsp olive oil
2 onions, chopped
2 cloves garlic, minced/or garlic powder if you prefer
4 cooked, boneless chicken breast halves, chopped
3 (14.5 oz) cans chicken broth
2 (4 oz) cans canned green chile peppers, chopped
2 tsp dried oregano
1½ tsp cayenne pepper
5 (15 oz) cans great northern beans with liquid
1 C shredded Monterey Jack cheese
Sour cream for topping

Heat the oil in a large pot over medium heat. Add the onions and garlic and sauté for 10 minutes, or until onions are tender. Add the chicken, chicken broth, green chile peppers, spices, and bring to a boil. Reduce heat to low and add the beans. Simmer 20-30 minutes, or until heated thoroughly. Pour into individual bowls and top with the cheese and sour cream.

My step-daughter loves this recipe almost as much as she loves dogs! 🌀

Watergate Salad

JULIE TRISTAN
Host, "Show Me St. Louis," KSDK-TV and Proud Stray Rescue Volunteer

1 (8 oz) tub whipped topping, thawed
1 small pack pistachio pudding
1 (20 oz) can crushed pineapple with juice
1 C mini-marshmallows
½ C pecans

Mix all together and refrigerate several hours prior to eating. May garnish halved cut cherries, if desired.

I first remember having this at my Grandma's House for Easter! Now it's another regular during the holidays and birthdays. Our family LOVES to make this! Sometimes I can convince myself that it's healthy…hey, it has pineapple in it! 🌀

Easy Vanilla Fruit Salad

CINDY COLLINS
Oldies 103.3 KLOU

3 (20 oz) cans pineapple chunks, drain and reserve pineapple juice
4 (15 oz) cans mandarin oranges, drained
2 (15 oz) cans peach chunks, drained
5 medium red apples, cut into 1-inch chunks (Fuji is best)
1 small jar of maraschino cherries, drained
2 (5.1 oz) packages instant vanilla pudding mix (sugar-free is fine)

Add enough cold water to the pineapple juice to make 3 cups of liquid. In a large bowl, whisk together the liquid and the pudding mix. This takes about 2 minutes. You want the pudding mix to be fully dissolved and starting to set up. Let stand an additional 2 minutes to set (do this in the refrigerator for best results). Add the fruit to the pudding mixture and toss/stir to combine. Refrigerate until well-chilled.

I keep all the ingredients (except apples) on hand in the pantry. We always have apples in the refrigerator, so I can whip this up with very little notice. It's cool, sweet, and fruity. Sometimes we serve it with the meal, sometimes as dessert. For an extra boost, serve toasted coconut on the side. I love it sprinkled on top of my serving of fruit salad. 🌀

Amish Lettuce Salad

LINDSEY SUDING
St. Louis Police Officer

½ head lettuce, chopped
1 small onion, chopped
4-6 hard-boiled eggs, chopped

Mix together and toss with dressing (recipe below) about 20 minutes before serving.

Dressing
1 C Miracle Whip® salad dressing
¼ C sugar
Dash of apple vinegar
Salt to taste (sweet to tart)

Mix together and toss with salad.

Recipe source: Myra Beachy, Arcola, Illinois

Officer Lindsey has assisted in the rescue of 80 dogs in the 8th District and helped with the prosecution of several animal abuse cases with Stray Rescue. You are a Stray Rescue of St. Louis Celebrity Officer Lindsey! 🌀

David's Delicious Salad

DAVID BACKES
St. Louis Blues

4 Romaine hearts
2 C baby spinach
1 Granny Smith apple
½ C sliced red globe grapes
½ red onion
½ red pepper
½ green pepper
½ C sweet cherry tomatoes
½ C raisins
¼ C thin strips of hot pepper cheese
¼ C candied walnuts
¼ C almond accents
Girard's® fat-free balsamic vinaigrette

Chop and slice Romaine into thin strips and Place into a large bowl. Add in baby spinach; do not slice. Chop the apples, grapes, onion, peppers, and tomatoes into bite-sized pieces and mix in with the Romaine and spinach. Sprinkle the raisins, cheese, walnuts, and almonds on top of the salad. Toss with dressing. ⊚

MaiN DiSHeS

BBQ Pork Stuffed Sweet Potato

JEN MYERS
Mornings/Music Director Y98

2 lbs pork loin
¼ C chili powder
2 Tbsp garlic salt
6 C Coke®
¾-1 C BBQ sauce
8 large sweet potatoes

Season pork with garlic salt and chili powder. Pour a little Coke in the bottom of the crock, and then add enough coke to just cover the pork loin. Cook on low for 8 hours. Preheat oven to 400°F. Scrub potatoes under water and wrap in foil. Bake at oven for about 60 minutes. Remove pork from crock-pot and discard Coke mixture, except for 2 Tbsp of juice. Shred the meat with a fork; mix with BBQ sauce and 2 Tbsp of juice. Leave slow cooker on low to keep things hot until you are ready to serve. Cut sweet potato open and fill with BBQ pork. Top with additional BBQ sauce.

Dan McLaughlin's Pork Tenderloin

DAN MCLAUGHLIN
Anchor, Fox Sports Midwest

6-8 strips of bacon
3-4 pork tenderloins, about 1 lb each
½ C soy sauce
1 Tbsp grated onion
1 clove garlic crushed
1 Tbsp vinegar
¼ tsp cayenne pepper
½ C sugar

Wrap bacon around tenderloins and fasten with wooden picks. Place meat in baking dish. Combine remaining ingredients and pour over meat. Let stand in refrigerator 4-5 hours, turning at least once. Preheat oven to 300°F. Roast in oven for 90 minutes until meat is 170°F. Reserve pan juices to spoon over meat. Serves 8-10.

Shrimp and Grits

ERIC KELLY
Executive Chef, Scape American Bistro

6 jumbo shrimp, peeled and deveined
1 Tbsp olive oil
1 Tbsp lemon juice
1 Tbsp Worcestershire
2 Tbsp hot sauce
4 Tbsp dark beer
4 Tbsp unsalted butter, diced
4 oz Cheddar Grits (recipe below)
2 tsp chives
Kosher salt, pepper, and BBQ spice to taste

Heat oil in sauté pan over moderate heat. Season shrimp with salt, pepper, and BBQ spice. Once oil is lightly smoking, carefully add shrimp and sauté 1 minute each side until pink and lightly caramelized. Remove shrimp to a warm holding platter. Degrease sauté pan and return to flame. Add lemon juice, Worcestershire, hot sauce and beer. Let mixture reduce by ¾. Remove from flame. Place grits in center of plate. Top with shrimp. Whisk butter into sauce reduction, and spoon sauce over shrimp and grits.

Cheddar Grits
1 C grits
2½ C chicken stock
2½ C heavy cream
3 oz shredded cheddar cheese

Place cream and stock in a small sauce pan. Over moderate heat, bring to a simmer. Slowly whisk in grits. Stir constantly for 12-15 minutes until cooked. Remove from heat and stir in cheddar. ◉

Chris' Catalina-Cranberry Chicken

CHRIS HIGGINS
Meteorologist, Fox 2 News

4-6 pre-cut chicken tenderloins or strips
1 (16 oz) can whole berry cranberry sauce
1 (8 oz) bottle Kraft® Classic Catalina dressing
1 envelope onion soup mix

Preheat oven to 350°F. Coat a 9x13 baking dish with non-stick cooking spray. Place chicken in prepared 9x13 baking dish. Mix remaining ingredients together and pour over the chicken. Bake 50 minutes or until chicken is done (165°F). Serves 4. ◉

Boeuf Bourguignon

RYAN DEAN
KSDK News Channel 5

½ lb bacon, diced
3 lbs chuck, cubed
⅓ C and 2 Tbsp flour, divided
4 Tbsp olive oil, divided
½ C brandy
6 Tbsp butter, divided
2 leeks, white part only, rinsed well, and diced
1 medium onion, minced
3 C carrots, quartered lengthwise if thick, then chopped into small chunks
3 tsp minced garlic
1 Tbsp tomato paste
1 (750 ml) Burgundy or Pinot Noir
1½-2 C beef broth
2 sprigs of thyme*
2½ Tbsp fresh chopped parsley
2 bay leaves
⅛ tsp ground cloves
Salt and pepper to taste
1 lb pearl onions**
1 lb cremini mushroom caps, quartered if small, or cut in 6-8 thick pieces if large
Egg noodles
Warm, crusty French bread
Butter

*dried is ok
**or buy already peeled, frozen onions and defrost earlier in the day

Preheat oven to 375°F. In large Dutch oven, cook bacon over medium heat until brown but not too crisp. Remove to plate with slotted spoon. Liberally salt and pepper beef cubes, then toss in plastic freezer bag with   cup flour to coat the pieces. Add 2 Tbsp olive oil to bacon grease in Dutch oven, brown meat in batches until brown on each side but not cooked through, a few minutes each side. Remove to plate with bacon using slotted spoon. Pour off excess fat, then add brandy to pot, deglaze while scraping up brown bits until consistency is thick and almost creamy. Pour this over meat and bacon, set aside. Add 2 Tbsp each olive oil and unsalted butter to pot. Once melted, add leeks and onion. Cook for 1-2 minutes before adding carrots; cook for another 3-4 minutes to allow carrots to soften. Add garlic, cook another 1-2 minutes. Add tomato paste, mix well. Add meat, bacon and juices from dish, mix well. Add wine, broth to cover the meat and vegetables, spices, and bring to a boil. Simmer covered on stove for 20 minutes, then place in oven for 60 minutes. After removing dish from oven, allow it to rest, covered, while preparing onions and mushrooms (or do this about 10 minutes before its scheduled to come out of oven).Melt 1 Tbsp butter in a 10-inch pan, cook onions until just browned, then add to stew. In same pan, melt an additional 1 Tbsp butter, sauté mushrooms until natural juices have evaporated, add to stew. Mix well, season as needed, simmer for 10 minutes. If it needs thickening, combine 1-2 Tbsp butter with same amount of flour, and slowly stir mixture into stew. 🌀

Rockin' Rik's Rockin' Rib Rub Recipe

RIK ANTHONY
WIL 92

⅔ C light brown sugar, packed

⅔ C granulated sugar

½ C paprika (smoked paprika recommended)

¼ C seasoned salt

¼ C onion salt

¼ C celery salt

2 Tbsp ground black pepper

2 Tbsp chili powder

2 tsp ground mustard powder

1 tsp ground ginger

½ tsp allspice

½-1 tsp cayenne pepper*

*use 1 tsp if you like it hot

Before cooking any of the meat, wash the skin thoroughly and pat dry with a paper towel. Apply a few drops of liquid smoke and hot sauce to the meat to get the party started. Rub liberally to the meat, making sure to coat everything. Combine all ingredients in a bowl and whisk until blended (be sure to get out any lumps). Transfer to an air-tight jar. This rub will keep for 30-60 days.

This rub is my personal favorite for baby back ribs, pork chops and chicken. I like to take the freshly rubbed meat and wrap it in plastic wrap and place in the refrigerator overnight. By morning, the brown sugar is making the meat happy, happy (as Emeril would say). Have a great BBQ season. ◎

Cajun-Baked Catfish

JANET AND LARRY CONNERS
News Anchor

2 C cornmeal

2 tsp salt

2 Tbsp pepper

8 (3-4 oz) catfish fillets, skin removed (optional)

2 Tbsp Cajun seasoning (Tony Cachere's® recommended)

¼ C butter or margarine, melted

Lemon wedges for garnish

Preheat oven to 400°F. Combine cornmeal, salt, and pepper. Dredge catfish fillets in cornmeal mixture; place fillets, skin sides down, on a greased baking sheet. You'll have plenty of cornmeal mixture for more fish, so keep coating those catfish and feed an army! Sprinkle Cajun seasoning over fillets. Drizzle with butter. A little extra melted butter that gathers on the sides of the fish will really crisp those bad boys right up! Bake 30 minutes or until golden and fish flakes with a fork. Garnish with lemon wedges or twists. Serves 8. ◎

Thai-Style Halibut with Coconut-Curry Broth

LEISA ZIGMAN
KSDK News Channel 5

4 (6 oz) pieces halibut fillet, skin removed
2 tsp vegetable oil
4 (about ¾ C) shallots, finely chopped
2½ tsp red curry paste*or 2 Tbsp curry powder
2 C low-sodium chicken broth
½ C light coconut milk
½ tsp salt (for mixture)
¼ tsp salt (for halibut)
Extra salt for seasoning
5 C baby spinach, steamed for 2 minutes or microwaved
½ C fresh cilantro leaves, coarsely chopped
2 scallions, green part only, thinly sliced
2 Tbsp fresh lime juice
Freshly ground black pepper
2 C cooked brown rice, for serving

*available in the Asian section of most supermarkets

In a large sauté pan, heat the oil over moderate heat. Add the shallots and cook, stirring occasionally, until beginning to brown, 3-5 minutes. Add the curry paste and cook, stirring, until fragrant, about 30 seconds. Add the chicken broth, coconut milk, ½ tsp salt and simmer until reduced to 2 C, about 5 minutes. Season the halibut with ¼ tsp salt. Arrange the fish in the pan and gently shake the pan so the fish is coated with the sauce. Cover and cook until the fish flakes easily with a fork, about 7 minutes. Arrange a pile of steamed spinach in the bottom of 4 soup plates. Top with the fish fillets. Stir the cilantro, scallions, and lime juice into the sauce and season, to taste, with salt and pepper. Ladle the sauce over the fish and serve with rice. Serves 4. ◎

McGonigle's Pork Loin

PAT MCGONIGLE
Co-anchor, KSDK News Channel 5

12 lbs pork loin
12 oz can of root beer
18 oz bottle of your favorite BBQ sauce
Hamburger or hot dog buns

Place the pork loin in a slow cooker. Pour in the root beer and barbecue sauce to cover the meat. Cook on low, 6-8 hours. Shred the meat and serve with hamburger or hot dogs buns. Serves an army. ◎

Penne Pasta with Sun Dried Tomatoes, Basil and Pine Nuts

FRANK CUSUMANO
Sports, KSDK News Channel 5

1 C sun-dried tomatoes
4 tsp pine nuts
½ C butter
4 C heavy cream (40%)
1 tsp salt
1 tsp white pepper
1 lb penne pasta, cooked al dente
2 C fresh basil, coarsely chopped
1 C Asiago cheese, grated

Reconstitute sun-dried tomatoes by soaking in hot water for 4 minutes. Drain, pat dry, and chop fine. Set aside. Lightly toast pine nuts in a dry skillet over medium heat. When the nuts start to color, immediately remove from heat; transfer to a small bowl. In a large saucepan, melt butter with cream, salt, and pepper. Simmer 5-10 minutes to reduce and thicken sauce. Add pasta, basil, and tomatoes. Toss to coat noodles with sauce. Add cheese and toss again. Cook until creamy, 3-4 minutes. Divide among pasta bowls and top with pine nuts. Serves 8.

Hawaiian-Style Fried Rice

JUSTIN HAIFLEY
Executive Chef, The Tavern

4 C cooked white rice
2 Tbsp rayu (sesame chili oil)
3 Tbsp shoyu
3 Tbsp oyster sauce
1 C "808" sausage, largely diced
1 lb bacon, rendered
4 eggs
¼ C green onion, diced
¼ C carrots, diced small
¼ C onion, diced small
¼ C peas
Fresh-cracked black pepper

Render bacon and sausage in a wok on high heat. Add sesame oil and cook rice until "toasted." Add vegetables and cook until tender. Stir in shoyu and oyster sauce and cook until rice is coated with sauce. Make a well in the middle of the wok and scramble eggs until cooked through. Add chopped green onion. Add black pepper. Mix until all ingredients are evenly distributed.

Jack's Rack of Lamb

BARRET JACKMAN
St. Louis Blues

½ (7-8 chops) rack of lamb
Freshly ground black pepper to taste
Salt to taste
½ tsp thyme
¼ C Dijon mustard
2-3 garlic cloves, finely chopped or garlic powder
½ C butter, melted
1-2 C fresh bread crumbs, crumbed in food processor, not seasoned or dried

Have butcher "French" the rack of lamb for roasting. Cover ends of bones with foil to prevent charring. Sprinkle lamb with thyme, pepper, and salt to taste. Preheat oven to 400°F. Place meat in roasting pan and bake 15 minutes. Remove and cool to handling temperature. Cover meat surface with mustard and sprinkle with garlic. Brush with melted butter. Coat the meat with bread crumbs. Return to roasting pan and cook 20 minutes more for medium-rare lamb chops. Allow to stand for 5 minutes, then carve. ◉

Spaghetti Pie

GUY PHILLIPS
Y98 Morning Show

6 oz spaghetti
1 tsp sugar
2 Tbsp butter
1 tsp crushed oregano
⅓ C grated Parmesan cheese
2 eggs, beaten well
½ tsp garlic salt
1 C cottage cheese
1 lb ground beef or pork sausage
½ C chopped onion
¼ C chopped green pepper
1 (8 oz) can cut up tomatoes
1 (6 oz) can tomato paste
½ C shredded mozzarella cheese

Preheat oven to 350°F. Cook spaghetti to package directions and drain (makes 3 cups). Stir butter into hot spaghetti. Stir in Parmesan cheese and eggs. Form spaghetti mix into a "crust" in a 10-inch pie plate. Spread cottage cheese on bottom of spaghetti crust. In skillet, cook ground beef or pork, onion, and green pepper until the veggies are tender and the meat is brown. Drain excess fat. Stir in undrained tomatoes, paste, sugar, oregano, and garlic salt; heat through. Turn meat mix into the spaghetti crust. Bake uncovered for 20 minutes. Sprinkle mozzarella on top and bake 5 minutes more or until the cheese melts. Remove from oven and let cool for 10-15 minutes. Cut into pie slices and serve! ◉

Char Sui Pork Steak

JUSTIN HAIFLEY
Executive Chef, The Tavern

Char Sui

2 lbs pork butt, cut into 4 pieces
3 Tbsp maltose*
3 Tbsp honey
3 Tbsp hoisin sauce
3 Tbsp sweet soy sauce
1 tsp Chinese five-spice powder
1 tsp white pepper
2 Tbsp sesame oil
8 cloves of garlic peeled and sliced
*available at most Asian grocery stores

Combine all the ingredients except the pork in a small sauce pan and simmer on medium heat until the maltose and honey are melted and the sauce is slightly thickened. Cool completely.

Brine

1 quart water
½ tsp curing salt
½ C brown sugar
3 Tbsp kosher salt
1 apple, diced
½ onion, diced
1 stalk celery, diced
1 tsp allspice berries
2 cloves
1 cinnamon stick
2 star anise
6 cloves garlic
12 peppercorns
6 bay leaves

Place ingredients in a large pot and bring to a simmer until the salt and sugar is dissolved. Cool overnight in refrigerator. Marinate 4 (16 oz) pork steaks in the brine for 48 hours. Remove from brine and pat dry. Place 1 pork steak in vacuum pack bag and add 2 oz char sui marinade. Repeat process for all four steaks. Vacuum pack pork. Cook pork steaks in thermal circulator at 145°F for 60 minutes. Cool pork steaks in ice bath for 60 minutes. Remove steaks from bag and brush with generous amounts of char sui marinade. Grill steaks on both sides until heated through. ◉

Ricotta Gnudi with Oxtail Ragout

JUSTIN HAIFLEY
Executive Chef, The Tavern

Gnudi

1 C Parmesan cheese
1 C ricotta cheese
2 eggs
1 egg yolk
1 tsp ground nutmeg
½ C all-purpose flour
2 tsp minced chives
1 Tbsp kosher salt
1 tsp fresh cracked black pepper
4 C semolina flour

In a large bowl, combine Parmesan, Ricotta, eggs, nutmeg, salt and pepper. Whip mixture until light and airy. Fold in flour and chives. Roll gnudi into 1-inch balls and place on a sheet tray. Cover gnudi balls completely with semolina flour and refrigerate overnight. Bring a large pot of water to a boil. Poach gnudi in water for about 5 minutes until they float to the top.

Oxtail Ragout

5 lbs oxtail
3 C ruby Port wine
2 onions, diced
2 stalks celery, diced
2 carrots, diced
6 bay leaves
2 Tbsp black peppercorns
1 bunch fresh thyme
6 C reduced veal stock

Sauté oxtails on each side in a braising pan until rendered crispy, remove from pan. Add celery, carrots, onion, bay leaf, thyme and peppercorns. Sauté for 5 minutes and then return oxtails to the braising pan. Add Port wine and cook for 5 minutes. Add veal stock and bring to a simmer. Remove pan from heat and place in a 300°F oven, uncovered. Cook oxtails turning every 30 minutes for about 2 hours or until tender and meat easily pulls off the bone. Remove oxtails from liquid and cook to room temperature. When oxtail is cooled, pick the meat from the bones. Meanwhile, reduce the braising liquid until it becomes a think sauce consistency and then strain through a fine mesh sieve. Add the oxtail to the sauce and keep warm. ⊚

Seasoned Pulled Pork

CHERISE PATTERSON
Owner/Operator 2 Girls 4 Wheels food truck

25 lbs pork butt
¼ C Sheries rib rub*
¼ C applewood smoke
1 Tbsp spoon cayenne pepper
1 Tbsp spoon brown sugar
1 Tbsp spoon mesquite seasoning
Dash of hickory salt
¼ C apple cider vinegar
*from Soulard Spice Market

Rub the pork butt until fully covered and pour in 1 cup water. Cook in a roasting pan on 300°F for 10 hours. Pull pork using 2 forks and serve with your favorite sauce and bread.

Parmesan Chicken

MARK (JAIME) BUEHRLE
Pitcher, Toronto Blue Jays

2 sleeves original Town House® crackers, crumbled
¼ C Parmesan cheese
1 C butter
1 lb of chicken breast strips
Pepper

Mix crackers and Parmesan cheese. Melt butter. Lightly pepper chicken. Dip in melted butter and roll in cracker mixture. Place chicken in 9x13 pan. Cook at 350°F for 15-20 minutes.

Roasted Free-Range Chicken

ANTHONY DEVOTI
Chef and Owner, FIVE Bistro

1 free-range chicken
Salt
Pepper
Favorite herb mixture*
Oil
Chicken stock

*herb mixture changes with the season; sage and rosemary are a good combination for fall

Split 1 chicken in half. (Benne's Farm free-range chickens recommended; a free-range bird really makes a difference in the taste and juices that result.) Salt and pepper the chicken, then rub with a mixture of herbs. Sear seasoned chicken in hot oil; skin side first, then turn on other side until all is golden brown. Place into a 450°F oven for 15 minutes; remove and turn the bird back to skin side and roast for 15 minutes more or until the juices run clear. The sauce is a combination of the deglazing of the skillet pieces, along with chicken stock or broth. ◉

Striped Bass Crudo with Blood Orange and Jalapeño

REX HALE
Chef, The Restaurant at the Cheshire Inn

10 oz skinless, striped bass fillet, blood line removed, very thinly sliced
2 blood oranges peeled, cut into segments, and cut in half
½ large jalapeño, seeded, rib removed, and finely, diced
6 Kalamata olives, pitted and finely, diced
20 baby arugula leaves
Juice of ½ blood orange
4 tsp high-quality extra virgin olive oil
Coarse sea salt and freshly ground black pepper to taste
Micro cilantro for garnish
Blood orange cut in 1/16 for garnish

Place 2½ oz of the thinly-sliced striped bass on the plate. Top with equal amount of blood orange wedges, minced jalapeño, and minced olives. Garnish each plate with arugula leaves. Drizzle with equal amounts of blood orange juice and extra virgin olive oil. Season the fish to taste with coarse sea salt and freshly ground black pepper and top with micro cilantro. Place a wedge of blood orange on the edge of the plate to garnish and add as additional juice for the dish. ◉

Beef and Cabbage

TAMMI MOOSHEGIAN
Program Director, SLU CME

2 lbs ground chuck or sirloin
1 very large white onion, sliced
2 large yellow peppers, seeded and sliced
1 very large head green cabbage or 2 small heads, cleaned, cut in quarters, cored, and sliced
1 (28 oz) large can crushed tomatoes
1 (15 oz) regular can tomato sauce
¼ C Country Bob's® steak sauce (optional)
1 Tbsp minced garlic
Salt and pepper to taste
1 Tbsp olive or canola oil

In large non-stick skillet heat oil, add onions and peppers. Sauté until tender, but not mushy. Add garlic, sauté for 2 more minutes on medium so garlic does not burn. Remove onions and peppers and set aside. Place ground meat in skillet and brown. Absorb grease from meat using paper towel. Add cabbage and can of crushed tomatoes, stir, cover and let cook 15 minutes. Stir, add tomato sauce, pepper and salt, stir. Add peppers and onions. Stir in optional Country Bob's steak sauce to give dish a rich dark sauce. Cook over low heat for 2 hours or pour into crock-pot and cook for 4 hours on high or 6-8 hours on low. Serve with corn bread. Add red pepper flakes or cayenne pepper for hot spicy version. Enjoy. Serves 8. ◉

Coca-Cola Ham

MANDY MURPHEY
Anchor, Fox 2 News

1 2-3 lb ham, fully-cooked, sliced
1 C brown sugar
1 (15.5 oz) can crushed pineapple
1 can Coca-Cola® (not diet)

Preheat oven to 325°F. Place ham in roaster or oven safe pan. Pack brown sugar on top of ham, pour pineapple, including juice, over ham. Pour coke over ham. Wrap tightly in aluminum foil. Bake at 325°F for 90 minutes per lb. For a smaller ham, bake at 350°F for 2 hours, turn oven off and let ham sit in oven and continue to cook. Serves 6-8. ◉

Enchilada Casserole

TOM O'NEAL
Fox 2 News

1 lb hamburger
Taco seasoning mix (1 envelope)
Shredded cheese, any variety
Corn tortillas
Butter
¼ C enchilada sauce
Salsa

Preheat oven to 350°F. Prepare hamburger and taco seasoning mix according to instructions on seasoning package. Warm tortillas in microwave until soft. Spread butter lightly on tortillas, fill with meat mixture and roll up. Place ¼ C enchilada sauce in 13x9 casserole dish. Place filled tortillas close together in casserole dish. Cover with cheese. Bake 20 minutes. Serve with salsa. ⦿

Bison Meatloaf

CHEF D. SCOTT
Balaban's Wine Cellar

2 lbs ground bison
3 garlic cloves, minced
2 eggs, lightly beaten
1 C raw bacon, finely chopped
I small sweet onion, minced
½ C panko bread crumbs
½ C grated Manchego cheese
1 Tbsp Worcestershire sauce
2 tsp kosher salt
1 tsp sage
1 tsp basil
1 tsp oregano

Preheat oven to 350°. Mix all ingredients together in large bowl. Your hands work best. Using small casserole dish coated with oil, pat Bison Mixture into pan as you would your own meatloaf recipe. Bake 90 minutes, covered in aluminum foil. Use your favorite meatloaf sauce or try Chef D. Scott's Favorite Meatloaf Sauce recipe below.

Chef D. Scott's Favorite Meatloaf Sauce
1 C catsup
½ C apple cider
¾ C brown sugar
2 Tbsp mustard
1 tsp kosher salt ⦿

The Ultimate St. Louis Style Pork Chop

TERRY BLACK
Co-founder of Super Smokers BBQ in Eureka, MO

Pork loin chop
Ground Italian sausage (2 parts ex: 2 C sausage)
Provolone cheese (1 part ex: 1 C cheese)
Favorite marinade (Super Smokers Mississippi Mud Sauce® recommended)
Favorite dry rub

Start with a pork loin chop that is about 1½ inches thick. Cut a slit large enough to stuff the chop with Italian sausage and Provolone cheese (like a pita pocket). Dip the chop in your favorite marinade. Then add your favorite dry rub to the outside of the chop. Use two parts Italian sausage to one part cheese and mix the two together. Stuff the mixture into the chop. Seal it up using toothpicks. Using indirect heat on a kettle-style smoker, this chop should be done and juicy in about 60 minutes. On a gas grill it will get done much faster, but a wood fire and charcoal gives it the best flavor.

St. Louis is known for its Italian food. Here is a pork chop that pays tribute to those who have loved and created St. Louis Italian-style food.

Terry Black is the co-founder of Super Smokers BBQ in Eureka, Missouri. It is the only restaurant in St. Louis ever to win the World BBQ Championship. Started in 1996, Super Smokers BBQ led the way in the revitalization of BBQ in St. Louis by introducing Competition Style BBQ to the market. It is the original and first of now several BBQ places in St. Louis cooking and serving BBQ with the championship attitude. ◎

Out-of-the-Doghouse Grilled Portabella

TERRY BLACK
Co-founder of Super Smokers BBQ in Eureka, MO

Portabella mushroom
Vinaigrette-style marinade or Super Smokers® Mississippi Mud sauce
Cooked meat or seafood
Mexican 4-cheese blend

Remove the stem from the middle of the portabella. Clean and rinse. Marinate in a vinaigrette-style marinade or Super Smokers BBQ Mississippi Mud sauce for just a couple of minutes. Pour off excess liquid, but leave just a little for flavor. Place chopped cooked meat or seafood (such as smoked chicken or very small shrimp—your choice) on the portabella. Top with four-blend cheese. It is most often called four-blend Mexican cheese. Cook using low temperature direct heat on a gas grill. In just a few minutes when cheese melts you are ready to eat. Serve immediately!

I cook these for my wife to get out of the doghouse sometimes. Works better than flowers. ◎

Roasted Sausages with Red Grapes

BILL KUNZ
Hwy 61 Roadhouse

2 pieces mild Italian sausages, 6-8 oz each
12 oz red seedless grapes
2 Tbsp olive oil
1 Tbsp balsamic vinegar
Salt to taste

Preheat oven to 475°F. Heat a cast-iron skillet over moderate heat until hot but not smoking. Lay the sausages in the skillet and cook them, turning once, until nicely browned, about 8 minutes total. While the sausages are cooking, remove the grapes from their stems, rinse under cool water, drain, place in a bowl, and toss them in olive oil. When the sausages are browned, place in an 8-inch square glass baking dish, and dump the grapes on top of and around them. Place dish in oven, and bake 25 minutes, turning the sausages once after about 15 minutes. Remove the pan from oven, and move the sausages to a platter. Pour the grapes and their juices into a small saucepan, season with a pinch of salt, and place the saucepan over medium-high heat, stirring, until the grapes bubble and sizzle and juices are syrupy. Remove the pan from the heat, stir in the vinegar. Pour the grapes over the sausages for service. Serve over mashed potatoes for an entrée or toasted bread for an appetizer. ⊚

Seared Duck Breast with Red Currant Sauce

AARON BAGGETT
Executive Chef, EdgeWild

2 duck breast halves
2 Tbsp butter
½ tsp minced garlic
¼ C finely chopped shallot
½ C chicken broth
¼ C red currant jam
¼ C orange juice
1 Tbsp honey

Using sharp knife, score skin in ¾-inch diamond pattern. Do not cut into flesh. Melt 1 Tbsp butter in heavy large skillet over medium-high heat. Sprinkle duck with salt and pepper. Add duck, skin side down, to skillet and cook until skin is browned and crisp, about 5 minutes. Turn duck breasts over, reduce heat to medium, and cook until browned and to desired doneness, about 6 minutes. Transfer to work surface, tent with foil to keep warm, and let rest for 10 minutes. Meanwhile, pour off all but 2 Tbsp drippings from skillet. Add shallot to skillet and stir over medium heat for 30 seconds, then add garlic and cook another 30 seconds. Add broth, jam, juice, and honey. Increase heat to high, and boil until sauce is reduced to glaze, stirring often, about 3 minutes. Whisk in 1 Tbsp cold butter. Season sauce to taste with salt and pepper. Thinly slice duck. Fan slices out on plates. Spoon sauce over and serve. Pair with EdgeWild Pinot Noir. ⊚

Portabella Sliders

BO MATTHEWS
Afternoon Host, 923 WIL

4-6 mini portabella mushrooms
2 slices of bacon, cooked and crumbled
1 C cooked chicken breast, cubed
1 tsp garlic
Liquid ranch dressing
Parmesan cheese
Mozzarella cheese

Preheat oven 350°F. Remove stems and 'fins' from portabella mushrooms and place, stem side up, on cookie sheet in heated oven for 10 minutes. In a bowl combine bacon, chicken and garlic. Cover above ingredients with liquid ranch dressing and sprinkle with Parmesan cheese. Remove mushrooms from oven; pour out and discard liquid from cap of mushroom. Top mushroom caps with chicken/bacon/ranch mixture. Sprinkle with mozzarella cheese and return to oven until cheese is melted. ⊚

Artichoke Frittata

CHRISTINE FELT
Producer, Fox Midwest

1 lb small red potatoes, cut into quarters
1 Tbsp + 1 tsp olive oil
2 green onions, sliced
1 (8 oz) orange pepper, chopped (optional)
1 pt grape tomatoes
1 (13-14 oz) can artichoke hearts, rinsed and chopped
4 large eggs + 4 large egg whites
½ C crumbled feta cheese

Arrange oven rack 6 inches from broiler. Preheat broiler. To microwave bowl, add potatoes and ¼ C water. Cover and vent with wrap and microwave on high for 8 minutes until tender. Drain. On baking sheet toss potatoes with 1 tsp oil and salt and pepper. Broil 6 minutes or until browned. Set aside.

In a non-stick skillet, heat 1 Tbsp of oil on medium. Add green onions and optional orange pepper. Cook 3 minutes until golden. Add tomatoes and artichoke hearts. Cook 2-5 minutes or until tomatoes start to burst. Stir occasionally. In medium bowl, beat eggs and egg whites with ¼ tsp salt and pepper and half of the feta. Pour over vegetables and tilt skillet to distribute evenly. Top with remaining feta. Cover and cook for 5-6 minutes or until set. Serve with potatoes. Serves 4. ⊚

Pot Roast with Porcini Mushrooms

JENNIFER BLOME
Anchor, News Channel 5

1 (5-lb) boneless beef chuck roast
Kosher salt and freshly ground black pepper
¼ C olive oil, divided
2 onions, chopped
6 cloves garlic, crushed
1 C red wine, such as Cabernet Sauvignon or Pinot Noir
1 (15 oz) can low-sodium beef broth + extra, as needed
½ oz dried porcini mushrooms
1 large sprig fresh rosemary, leaves removed and chopped
6 sprigs fresh thyme, leaves removed and chopped

Preheat oven to 350°F. Pat the beef dry with paper towels, and season with salt and pepper. In a heavy 6-quart pot or Dutch oven, heat 2 Tbsp of oil over medium-high heat. Add the beef and cook until browned on all sides, about 12 minutes. Remove the beef and set aside. Reduce the heat to medium. Add the remaining oil and the onions. Cook, stirring frequently, until tender, about 8 minutes. Add the garlic and cook for 1 minute until aromatic. Add the wine and scrape up the brown bits that cling to the bottom of the pan with a wooden spoon. Stir in the broth and mushrooms. Return the beef to the pot and bring the liquid to a boil. Cover the pot and transfer to oven. Cook until the beef is fork-tender, about 3 hours, turning the beef over halfway through and adding more beef broth, as needed. Transfer the beef to a cutting board. Tent with foil and let stand for 15 minutes. Meanwhile, spoon any excess fat off the top of the pan juices. Using an immersion blender, blend the pan juices and vegetables until smooth. Add the rosemary and thyme. Bring sauce to a simmer for 5 minutes. Salt and pepper to taste. Cut the beef into 1-inch pieces and place on a platter. Spoon some of the sauce over the meat and serve the remaining sauce on the side. The cooked pan juices and vegetables can also be pureed in a blender. ◉

Crab Cakes

JENNIFER BLOME
Anchor, News Channel 5

8 saltine crackers, crumbled
1 Tbsp mayonnaise
1 Tbsp Worcestershire sauce
1 tsp Old Bay® seasoning
¼ tsp salt
1 egg, beaten
1 lb lump crabmeat

Mix mayonnaise, Worcestershire sauce, Old Bay, salt, egg, and crabmeat. Mix lightly and shape into 4 patties. If time permits, refrigerate patties 30 minutes to help keep them together when cooking. Broil or fry until golden-brown on both sides. ◉

Spicy Honey Chicken

JENNIFER BLOME
Anchor, News Channel 5

2 tsp garlic powder
2 tsp chili powder
1 tsp ground cumin
1 tsp paprika
½ tsp ground red pepper
8 skinless, boneless chicken thighs
Non-stick cooking spray
6 Tbsp honey
3 tsp cider vinegar

Preheat oven to 400°F. Combine first 6 ingredients in a large bowl. Add chicken to bowl; toss to coat. Mix honey and vinegar together. Pour over chicken. Roast at 400°F for 35-40 minutes. ◎

Imam Bayilde

MEHMET YILDIZ
Executive Chef, Aya Sofia

4 small Chinese eggplants
5 Tbsp extra virgin olive oil
8 cloves garlic, crushed
1 medium white onion, finely chopped
4 oz sundried tomatoes
1 lb cherry tomatoes, cut in half
2 tsp sugar
Salt and black pepper to taste
Juice of ½ lemon
Handful of chopped fresh parsley or basil

Preheat oven to 350°F. Cut eggplants in half lengthwise. Slit down the middle so that there is room to place stuffing. In a large sauté pan, cook eggplants in 2 Tbsp olive oil until soft. Turn eggplants over and repeat. Remove from pan, arrange eggplants in baking dish, and let cool. Keep oil in pan for re-use.

In same pan heat 2 additional Tbsp of olive oil. Sauté garlic first, then add chopped onions, sundried tomatoes, cherry tomatoes, sugar, salt, and black pepper. Cook 5-7 minutes over high heat then remove from heat. Once mixture has cooled, add lemon juice and stir. Stuff into eggplants. Bake 15-20 minutes. Sprinkle parsley or basil on top of eggplants as garnish. Drizzle a bit more olive oil before serving. Serve warm or at room temperature.

This recipe is a traditional Turkish recipe that dates back to the Middle Ages. The Turkish priest (Imam) fainted because of the amount of delicious and expensive olive oil that was used in the preparation of this dish. ◎

Seared Wild Halibut with Succotash and Sherry Vinegar Glaze

REX HALE
Chef, 360

6 Tbsp unsalted butter
36 roasted, peeled pearl onions
¾ C half-rendered, thick-cut smoked bacon
1½ C corn kernels, freshly shucked
18 heirloom cherry tomatoes, halved
1½ C crowder peas, cleaned
2 Tbsp minced fresh garlic
3 oz hard apple cider
3 oz heavy cream
3 oz grated Parmesan
Sea salt and freshly ground black pepper to taste
1 oz micro basil
6 (4 oz) center-cut halibut fillets
Sherry vinegar glaze and extra virgin olive oil

Season fillets and sear over high heat in 2 Tbsp olive oil while cooking to medium done. Sauté vegetables, bacon, and garlic in butter. Deglaze with hard apple cider and add cream. Reduce and add Parmesan cheese and season to taste with salt and pepper. Add micro basil. When the fish is cooked, rest the fillets on top of the succotash. Drizzle the plate with sherry vinegar glaze and extra virgin olive oil and garnish with micro basil. ◉

BREADS

Parmesan POP Biscuits

LAUREN "LERN" COLVIN
On-Air Personality, KSHE 95

3 eggs
¾ C all-purpose flour
¼ tsp salt
½ tsp freshly ground black
½ tsp herbs de provence
4 Tbsp chopped fresh parsley
1 C skim milk or whole milk
¾ C (about 5 oz) grated Parmesan
¼ C Parmesan cheese to sprinkle on top

Preheat oven to 400°F. In a medium mixing bowl, beat together eggs, flour, salt, pepper, herbs, milk, and cheese. Blend on medium speed. Spray a mini-muffin pan with non-stick cooking spray. Pour batter into muffin cup, filling each ¾ full. Top with Parmesan cheese before baking. Bake until puffed and golden brown, 20-25 minutes. Remove from muffin pan and let cool. Serves 12. ◉

Bacon Muffins

CASSIE VIRES
Home Wine Kitchen

2 slices bacon, chopped finely
2 C all-purpose flour
2¼ tsp baking powder
½ tsp salt
2 Tbsp light brown sugar
1 egg
1 C whole milk
2 Tbsp bacon drippings, melted

Preheat oven to 425°F. Grease, or spray with non-stick cooking spray, a 12-cup muffin tin, or line with paper liners. Pan fry the chopped bacon in a small, heavy saucepan until crispy. Remove with a slotted spoon and let cool slightly. In a large bowl, whisk the flour, baking powder, salt, and light brown sugar together until well-combined. Add bacon pieces and stir until they are well distributed and coated in the flour mixture. Lightly beat the egg in a medium bowl. Add the milk and the bacon drippings and stir to combine. Add the milk mixture to the dry ingredients all at once. Stir quickly until just combined, then stir 5-6 more times until well-blended. Do not stir until smooth. Drop batter by spoonfuls into the greased muffin tin, filling each cup ⅔ full. Bake 20 minutes, or until lightly browned. Makes 12 muffins. ◉

Chef Pam's Rosemary Focaccia

PAM SMITH
Chef, Your Home Bistro

4 C bread flour
2 Tbsp sugar
1½ tsp salt
1½ Tbsp instant yeast
¼ C fresh rosemary, chopped
1-2 Tbsp olive oil
1½-2 C water
Kosher salt
Cornmeal

Place dry ingredients and rosemary in the work bowl of a food processor and blend briefly to combine. While the food processor is running, gradually add oil and water and mix until the dough forms a ball. Continue to mix for 30-60 seconds to develop the dough. Remove the dough, shape into a ball, and place it in a greased bowl. Cover with a towel or plastic wrap. Let the dough rise for 1-2 hours.

Punch the dough down and shape it into a disk. Cover it and allow it to rest for a few minutes. Spread the dough into a 12-14-inch round, flat piece. Place it on a baking sheet that has been dusted with cornmeal. Coat the top with olive oil and sprinkle with kosher salt. Preheat oven to 375°F. When the dough has doubled in height, bake 20-25 minutes. The crust should be golden brown and the loaf should sound hollow when tapped. Makes 1 loaf.

Vegan Banana-Espresso-Chocolate Chip Muffins

REINE BAYOC
Sweetart

1¾ C mashed banana
½ C agave syrup
¼ C brown sugar
½ C safflower oil or coconut oil
¼ C almond or soy milk, unsweetened
1 Tbsp apple cider vinegar
1 Tbsp flax meal mixed with 2 Tbsp water
1½ C whole-wheat pastry flour
2 tsp espresso powder
1½ tsp baking soda
½ tsp sea salt
1 C semi-sweet chocolate chips

Preheat oven to 350°F. Line a 12-cup muffin pan with paper liners. In a medium bowl, stir together the bananas, agave, brown sugar, almond or soy milk, apple cider vinegar, and flax meal solution.

In another bowl, whisk together the flour, instant espresso powder, baking soda, and salt. Make a well in the middle of the dry ingredients. Pour the wet ingredients into the well and fold until just combined. Fold in the chocolate chips. Fill each liner ¾ full (about 2 oz each). Bake 15-20 minutes or until a toothpick inserted in the center of a muffin comes out clean. Cool for 15 minutes. These muffins can be stored in an air-tight container at room temperature for 3 days or frozen for 3 months.

Pineapple Zucchini Bread

COREEN SAVITSKI
Show me St. Louis

3 eggs
1 tsp vanilla
2 C peeled grated and drained zucchini
2 C sugar
1 C oil
3 C flour
1 tsp salt
1½ tsp cinnamon
2 tsp soda
½ tsp baking powder
¾ tsp nutmeg
1 C walnuts
1 C crushed pineapple, drained

Preheat oven to 325°F. Grease and prepare two loaf pans. Sprinkle bottoms of pans with a cinnamon and sugar mixture. In large mixing bowl, beat eggs until fluffy. Add sugar, vanilla, oil, and zucchini. Blend well. In a separate bowl, mix together the dry ingredients with walnuts and pineapple. Add to egg mixture blending well. Pour into prepared loaf pans. Bake 60 minutes or until nicely browned. Makes 2 loaves.

Recipe from the kitchen of Julia R. Cihak (aka Mary Ann Cihak, Coreen's mother)

Savory Scones

CHRISTY AUGUSTIN
Pint Size Bakery

3½ C unbleached, all-purpose flour
2 tsp kosher salt
¼ C granulated sugar
1½ Tbsp baking powder
2 Tbsp fresh herbs, finely chopped
1 tsp black pepper, freshly ground
⅔ cold, unsalted butter-cubed
½ C veggies and/or meat of your choice
¼ C grated or cubed cheese
1⅓ C buttermilk
Egg wash and Parmesan cheese to finish

Combine all dry ingredients into a large bowl and whisk to lighten. Add cold butter to the flour mixture and work the butter in by hand until the butter is the size of peas and hazelnuts (similar to making pie dough or biscuits). Add flavor ingredients and gently stir in the buttermilk. Be careful not to over mix nor thoroughly moisten the dough. It will be a little dry and shaggy. Refrigerate for 30 minutes. After the dough has chilled, roll or pat it out on a floured work surface, then fold it in half, roll it out again to a thickness of approximately 2 inches, and then fold in half again. Using plenty of flour, roll the dough to a thickness of 1-inch. Using a round or square cutter portion the scones and place on a parchment lined sheet tray. Bake now or freeze the dough for later. Preheat oven to 375°F. Before baking, brush the scone with an egg wash mixture of 2 whole eggs and 2 Tbsp of milk, then sprinkle with Parmesan cheese. Bake 20 minutes or more until lightly golden and firm to the touch.

This recipe can be really versatile in flavor. Combinations we do at Pint Size are bacon-blue cheese-caramelized onion, spinach-artichoke-Asiago, ham-cheddar-green onion, sun dried tomato-mozzarella-basil, etc. ◎

Davidson's Great Glazed Pumpkin Loaf

JOHN DAVIDSON
Former President, St. Louis Blues

6 oz whipped cream cheese
¼ C butter
1¼ C sugar
2 eggs
1 C canned pumpkin
1¾ C flour
1 tsp baking soda
¼ tsp baking powder
1 tsp cinnamon
½ tsp ground cloves
½ C chopped walnuts

Glaze
½ C powdered sugar
1 Tbsp milk
¼ tsp ground cloves
¼ tsp ground nutmeg

Preheat oven to 350°F. Place cream cheese, butter, and sugar in a mixing bowl and cream together. Beat in eggs one at a time until well-blended. Mix in pumpkin. In another bowl, combine all 7 remaining ingredients. Stir until thoroughly mixed. Pour all at once over batter and stir until just moistened. Turn into greased 9x5x3 loaf pan. Bake 60 minutes. Cool 10 minutes. For the glaze, mix all glaze ingredients and poke holes in the top of the loaf. Pour glaze all over the top of the warm loaf. Let sit for 60 minutes in the pan, then remove.

This is a loaf the Davidson family eats every Thanksgiving and Christmas. ◉

Desserts

Bummies Sugar Cookies

JULIE TRISTAN
Host, "Show Me St. Louis" KSDK and Proud Stray Rescue Volunteer

1 tsp baking soda
1 Tbsp vinegar
1 C butter or margarine
1 C brown sugar, packed
1 C white sugar
2 eggs
1 tsp vanilla
4 C flour
Colored sugars and decorations

Preheat oven to 375°F. Dissolve baking soda in vinegar in small dish. In large bowl, mix butter with sugars, then add eggs, vanilla, soda, and vinegar. Mix in flour one cup at a time. Dough gets stiffer.

If needed, chill in refrigerator for 30-60 minutes. Pinch off a little at a time; roll out on floured surface or waxed paper to about ¼-inch thickness. Cut with cookie cutters that you first dip in flour. Decorate with colored sugars. Bake on aluminum foil or greased cookie sheet for 7 minutes. Baking time depends on how thick or thin the dough is rolled, and if you like crisp or soft cookies. They harden upon cooling, so don't overcook if you like softer cookies.

Even as an adult I make these with Momma Tristan every year before Christmas! This is a perfect sugar cookie recipe to use with cookie cutters and to decorate with red hots, sprinkles, etc. Make sure you leave enough dough at the end to make a "hand" cookie cut out!

Key Lime Pie

CYRANO'S RESTAURANT

2 cans of sweetened condensed milk
5 egg yolks
1 C key lime juice
1 baked graham cracker crust

Mix sweetened condensed milk with egg yolks, add key lime juice and whisk until incorporated. Pour filling into crust and bake at 325°F for 10 minutes. Cool in refrigerator at least 60 minutes before cutting.

Faux Cinnamon Baked Apples

SHERRY FARMER
Oldies 103.3 KLOU

3 zucchinis, seeded and cut into slices
12 oz jar Walden Farms® apple butter
12 oz jar Walden Farms® caramel
12 oz jar Walden Farms® chocolate syrup (optional)
Cinnamon
Lemon juice
Glass bowl

Preheat oven to 350°F. Prepare a baking dish with cooking spray. Place the zucchini slices into a bowl and drizzle with a little lemon juice. Stir in several large spoonfuls of apple butter. Mix and spread on prepared baking dish. Sprinkle with cinnamon and then drizzle with desired amount of caramel syrup. Bake 30 minutes or until the faux apples are at the desired tenderness. Sprinkle with more cinnamon once out of oven and enjoy! Serves 8-10.

If you are having a chocolate craving, drizzle some chocolate syrup on top too. However, you might want to wait until it cools down a bit because the juices get thicker. ◎

Marshy Pie

RON "JOHNNY RABBITT" ELZ
Host of Route 66 on Saturday Nights, KMOX/CBS Radio

1 C sugar
¼ C cornstarch
⅛ tsp salt
½ C butter
2 C whole milk
1 tsp vanilla
¼ tsp nutmeg

Preheat oven to 325°F. Mix sugar, cornstarch, and salt with milk and butter in saucepan. Add vanilla and nutmeg. Cook slowly, stirring constantly until thick-about 12-15 minutes. Pour into baked pie shell and sprinkle lightly with more nutmeg. Bake 10 minutes.

Marshmallow was our neighbors dog, and when they went away for trips, my happy assignment was to take care of Marshy. Then after their return, Judith would make us a sugar cream pie that we called Marshy Pie. Marshy is no longer with us, but we still get an occasional Marshy Pie and it brings back fond memories. ◎

No Bake Energy Balls

JILL DEVINE
Y98 Mid-Days/Fresh 102.5 and Program Coordinator, Y98

1 C dry oatmeal (old-fashioned oats recommended)
⅔ C coconut (organic, unsweetened recommended)
½ C peanut butter (all natural, unsweetened peanut butter recommended)
½ C ground flaxseed
½ C dark chocolate chips (optional)
⅓ C honey
1 tsp vanilla extract

Stir all ingredients together in a medium bowl until thoroughly mixed. Let chill in the refrigerator for 30 minutes. When chilled, roll into ping-pong-ball-sized balls. Store in air-tight container and keep refrigerated for up to 1 week. Makes 20-25 cookies.

Strawberry Yogurt Pie

TOM O'NEAL
Fox 2 News

1 lb fresh strawberries, sliced
2-5 (3 oz) containers of Oikos® Greek* strawberry yogurt, or yogurt of choice
8 oz container of whipped topping**
1 pre-made graham cracker pie crust

*Greek works better because it's thicker

**light or fat-free not recommended

Combine yogurt and whipped topping. Mix in approximately ¾ of the strawberries. Pour combined ingredients into graham cracker crust. Top with the remainder of sliced strawberries. Refrigerate for 2-3 hours to set. Best when eaten within a couple of days as crust may get soggy.

Peanut Butter Surprise

MELANIE MOOSHEGIAN
Fox Sports Midwest

2 (24 oz) packages of white almond bark*
1 C crunchy peanut butter
3 C mini marshmallows
3 C Rice Krispies® cereal
2 C Spanish peanuts
*do not use white chocolate

Line table or counter top with about 4 feet of waxed paper. In a large bowl, mix dry ingredients and set aside. Place almond bark in a large, glass microwaveable bowl. Heat for 2 minutes and stir. Continue heating in 30 second increments until smooth. Do not overcook. It will burn easily. Once smooth, stir in crunchy peanut butter, then pour mixture over dry ingredients and stir. Drop by rounded Tbsp onto waxed paper, but work quickly as it will set up and dry fast! Break into pieces. Makes about 80 cookies.

This one of my all-time favorite candies, especially around Christmas! Enjoy. 🌀

Red Velvet Cake

BISTRO 1130

2½ C all-purpose flour
2 C sugar
1 Tbsp cocoa powder
1 tsp baking soda
1 Tbsp vinegar
2 eggs
1½ C vegetable oil
1 tsp vanilla extract
1 Tbsp red food coloring
1 C buttermilk

In a large bowl, combine the dry ingredients and whisk until thoroughly blended. In a separate bowl, beat the eggs until frothy and pale yellow, then add the rest of the wet ingredients. Add the wet ingredients to the dry ingredients in 3 increments, beating until just blended. Bake at 350°F, 35-45 minutes or until a toothpick inserted in the center comes out clean. Frost with your favorite icing. 🌀

Crème Brûlée Bread Pudding

LEON CRUES
Chef, Wild Flower Restaurant and Catering

3 C granulated sugar
15 egg yolks
1 quart heavy cream (40%)
1 Tbsp pure vanilla extract
½ Tbsp cinnamon
½ tsp nutmeg
1 loaf (16 slices) cubed Texas toast

Preheat oven to 350°F. Grease a 13x9x2 pan. Placed cubed bread in pan. Sprinkle the cinnamon and nutmeg onto the bread. Mix together granulated sugar, eggs, and heavy cream in a bowl; add vanilla extract. Pour mixture over cubed bread and let it sit in the refrigerator for 30 minutes. Cover bread pudding with foil. Bake 2 hours in a water bath, half-sheet tray, or until set. For the last 20 minutes remove the foil and bake until golden brown. Then place on cooling rack.

Caramel Sauce
½ C butter
1 C light brown sugar
¼ tsp salt
1 tsp vanilla
½ C evaporated milk

In a sauce pan over medium heat, melt butter and brown sugar. Bring to a boil and remove from heat. Whisk in salt, vanilla, and evaporated milk. The sauce can be made ahead, and then warmed in the microwave. Cut cooled bread pudding into squares and then top each with warm caramel sauce. ◎

Cole's Creamy Coconut Cake

SANDY MILLER
News Anchor, Fox 2

1 (16 oz) package white cake mix
1 (14 oz) can cream of coconut
1 (14 oz) can sweetened condensed milk
1 (16 oz) container frozen whipped topping, thawed
1 (10 oz) package flaked coconut

Preheat oven to 350°F. Prepare cake according to package directions. Bake in a 9x13 pan. Cool completely. In a small bowl combine cream of coconut and condensed milk. Poke holes in cake with a straw. Pour milk mixture over cake and spread with whipped topping. Sprinkle coconut over cake. Serve chilled.

This is my son Cole's favorite cake. He requests it every year for his birthday. ◎

Melanie's Baklava

MELANIE MOON
News Anchor, KPLR TV

2 packages frozen phyllo pastry, thawed
2½ C butter, melted
1½ C flaked coconut, lightly toasted
½ C finely chopped macadamia nuts, toasted
¾ C pecans, finely chopped
1½ C brown sugar, firmly packed
1 tsp ground allspice
1½ C sugar
½ C water
½ C honey

Butter a 13x9x2 baking pan. Cut phyllo in half crosswise, and cut each half to fit pan. Discard trimmings. Cover phyllo with a slightly damp towel. Layer 10 sheets of phyllo in pan, brushing each sheet with melted butter. Combine coconut, macadamia nuts, pecans, brown sugar, and allspice; stir well. Sprinkle ⅓ of nut mixture over phyllo in pan. Top with 10 sheets of phyllo, brushing each sheet with melted butter. Repeat procedure twice with remaining nut mixture. Top with 10 sheets of phyllo, brushing each sheet with melted butter. Repeat procedure twice with remaining nut mixture, phyllo, and butter, ending with buttered phyllo. Cut into diamond shapes, using a sharp knife. Bake at 350°F for 45 minutes or until top is browned. Let cool completely. Combine 1½ C sugar, water, and honey in a medium saucepan. Bring to a boil; reduce heat, and simmer 5 minutes. Remove from heat; drizzle syrup over baklava. Cover and let stand at room temperature 24 hours. Makes about 3 dozen.

Salted Caramel Ice Cream Pie

DIERBERGS SCHOOL OF COOKING

1 (9 oz) box chocolate-covered pretzels,* divided
3 Tbsp Dierbergs butter, melted and slightly cooled
½ gallon Dierbergs vanilla ice cream
⅔ C caramel ice cream topping
¾ tsp coarse salt
*can be found in the produce department

Reserve 8 pretzels for garnish. Place remaining pretzels in work bowl of food processor fitted with steel knife blade; process until finely chopped (about 1¾ C). Add butter; pulse until crumbs hold together. Press mixture evenly onto bottom and up sides of 9inch deep-dish pie plate. Freeze until set, about 20 minutes. Scoop ⅔ of the ice cream into balls and arrange in prepared pie crust; press and swirl with back of spoon. Microwave caramel topping in 15-second intervals until pourable consistency. Drizzle half of the caramel topping over ice cream. Repeat layers with remaining ice cream and topping. Freeze until firm, at least 4 hours. Let pie stand at room temperature 10 minutes. Cut into wedges, sprinkle salt over top, and garnish with reserved pretzels.

Cindy's Chocolate Chip Weather Cookies

CINDY PRESZLER
Chief Meteorologist, KSDK News Channel 5

1 C softened shortening
¾ C brown sugar, firmly packed
¾ C granulated sugar
1 tsp vanilla
½ tsp water
2 eggs
2 C flour*
1 tsp baking soda
1 tsp salt
1 C chopped nuts
1 package chocolate chips
*if humidity is high outside, use more flour; if it is low, use 2 C

Preheat oven to 375°F. Beat shortening, sugars, vanilla, water, and eggs until light and fluffy.

Mix flour with soda and salt. Blend into a mixture. Stir in nuts if you like. Use 2 or 3 different kinds of chips, if preferred, including semi-sweet, milk, and dark. Drop onto a greased baking sheet and bake 10 minutes or until done. ☺

Beachy Crunch

LINDSEY SUDING
St. Louis Police Officer

1½ lb white chocolate bark
2 Tbsp cooking oil
2 C Rice Krispies® cereal
2 C Kix® cereal
2 C small marshmallows
2 C toasted pecans
Pretzels to desired amount:

Melt white chocolate bark and cooking oil together. Add all ingredients together and place on buttered waxed paper. If there is too much white chocolate, add more pretzels. Cool. Store in covered container

Grandma Myra and Grandpa Larry make this every Christmas for our stockings.

Officer Lindsey has assisted in the rescue of 80 dogs in the 8th District and helped with the prosecution of several animal abuse cases with Stray Rescue. You are a Stray Rescue of St. Louis Celebrity Officer Lindsey! ☺

Cherry Cake Cobbler

LINDSEY SUDING
St. Louis Police Officer

1 package Duncan Hines® white cake mix
1¼ C water
⅓ C cooking oil
3 eggs
1 C sugar
2 Tbsp cornstarch
2-16 oz pitted red tart cherries with liquid
2 Tbsp melted margarine
½ tsp red food coloring
¾ tsp almond extract

Preheat oven to 350°F. Mix cake mix, water, oil, and eggs. Stir together cherry mixture, including sugar, pitted red tart cherries, margarine, red food coloring, and almond extract. Grease and flour 13x9 cake pan. Add cake batter to cake pan. Spoon cherry mixture evenly over cake batter. Bake 50-60 minutes or until golden brown. Serve warm or cold with whipped topping or ice cream.

From Jeanette Suding, Arcola Illinois

Officer Lindsey has assisted in the rescue of 80 dogs in the 8th District and helped with the prosecution of several animal abuse cases with Stray Rescue. You are a Stray Rescue of St. Louis Celebrity Officer Lindsey! ⦾

Mud Pie

SUGARFIRE SMOKEHOUSE

8 Tbsp butter
1 C chocolate chips
3 Tbsp white corn syrup
2 Tbsp sour cream
3 eggs
1 C granulated sugar
1 graham cracker crust

In a saucepan melt butter, chocolate chips, and corn syrup. Heat until chocolate and butter are melted. Remove from heat and whisk in 3 eggs and one C sugar. Mix in the sour cream. Pour filling into crust and bake at 325°F for 30 minutes or until puffed. Serve cold or at room temperature. ⦾

Grilled Strawberry Shortcake

DIERBERGS SCHOOL OF COOKING

1 (16 oz) box strawberries, sliced
2 Tbsp Dierbergs granulated sugar
4 slices angel food cake or pound cake, sliced ¾-inch thick
3 Tbsp peach schnapps, divided
½ C heavy whipping cream
2 Tbsp Dierbergs powdered sugar

In medium bowl, combine strawberries and granulated sugar; cover and chill at least 60 minutes. Brush cut sides of cake with 2 Tbsp of the liqueur. Place cake on oiled grid over medium heat; grill until grill marks appear, 1-2 minutes per side. In large mixer bowl, beat whipping cream, powdered sugar, and remaining 1 Tbsp liqueur at high speed until soft peaks form. Place cake slices on individual plates; divide strawberries along with juice over tops. Serve with dollop of sweetened whipped cream.

Southern Sour Cream Pound Cake

CASSADY CALDWELL
Luvy Duvy's Cafe

1 C butter
2⅔ C sugar
6 eggs, beat one at a time
3 C plain flour
¼ tsp of salt
8 oz container of sour cream
¼ tsp of baking soda

Melt butter, set aside. Combine sugar, flour, and salt in one bowl, set aside. Mix in the baking soda with sour cream. Beat eggs in one big bowl then add in butter, dry ingredients, and sour cream mix. Bake at 300°F for 60 minutes. Turn off oven and let it finish off for 15 minutes in oven. Top with whipped cream, ice cream, strawberries, blueberries, or whatever you like!

Perfect on a hot summer day!

Crème Cheese Cookies

KELLY JACKSON
KSDK News Channel 5

½ C butter
1 (3 oz) package cream cheese, room temperature
¾ C sugar
1 egg yolk
1 tsp vanilla
½ tsp baking powder
¼ tsp salt
2 C flour
½ C nuts (optional)

Preheat oven 350°F. Mix well the butter, softened cream cheese, sugar, egg yolk, vanilla, salt, and baking powder. Slowly add flour until mixed well, followed by optional nuts. Spray cookie sheet with non-stick cooking spray. Roll a teaspoon size of batter into a ball and place on cookie sheet. Use a fork to flatten each rolled cookie to make a crisscross design with a fork. Continue until the sheet is full. Bake 6-8 minutes. The cookie will not brown on top, so check the bottom.

My mother used to make these every year during the holidays. Growing up, I was her little shadow, so I'd always be in the kitchen with her, watching how she made everything and luckily I picked up some of her culinary skills. I loved these cookies and to this day, my sister and I make them at Christmas time. I've made them once "off-season," and they just didn't taste the same! They are easy to make, so I hope the readers will have their little ones help them make these easy and wonderfully delicious cookies too. They taste best during the holidays and with a cup coffee or tea. ◎

Warm Chocolate Soufflé Cake

REX HALE
Chef, The Restaurants of the Cheshire Inn

1 lb, 6 oz bittersweet chocolate
5 oz butter
12 eggs, separated
11 oz sugar
1 oz Grand Marnier®
3 Tbsp cornstarch

Melt chocolate and butter together. Add half of sugar, Grand Marnier, and cornstarch to egg yolks. Whisk mixture until smooth. Whip the egg whites with the remaining half of sugar until soft peaks are formed. Spray 3-inch stainless rings or cup with non-stick cooking spray. Preheat oven to 350°F. Mix chocolate and butter mixture with egg yolks and whites; fold together. Spoon the mixture into cups and bake 9-12 minutes until cake sets on the outside but is still soft in the center. Allow to cool. Serve with seasonal ice cream. ◎

Strawberry Shortcake

REX HALE
Chef, The Restaurants of the Cheshire Inn

3 C cake flour
1 C sugar
1½ Tbsp baking powder
1 tsp salt
¾ C whipped butter
3 eggs
¼ C milk
2 Tbsp vanilla extract

Mix all dry ingredients. Cut butter into the flour. Whip eggs lightly. Add the eggs and milk, blending until smooth. Refrigerate for at least 30 minutes. When chilled place shortcake dough on well-floured surface. Roll or pat it with hands. Cut with a biscuit cutter into 6 4-inch shortcakes. Place on greased baking sheet. Preheat oven to 350°F. Bake shortcakes for 12 minutes. Slice in half just out of oven. Spoon the strawberry filling on the bottom half of the shortcakes. Top with whipped cream. Dust the top crust with powdered sugar and garnish with a mint sprig.

Strawberry Filling
3½ pints strawberries, cleaned and hulled
1 C sugar
2 Tbsp Grand Marnier®

Slice 2½ pints strawberries. Puree the remaining pint of strawberries in a food processor with the sugar and Grand Marnier. Pour over sliced berries and fold together. To serve: whip 2 C whipping cream with ¼ C sugar.

♥ FRiENDS RECIPES ♥

Josephine

EGGS AND BREAKFAST CASSEROLES

Breakfast Cups

KATHLEEN KAMINSKY

1 (24 oz) bag of shredded hash browns
2 tsp salt
1 tsp pepper
2 Tbsp oil
⅓ C shredded cheddar cheese + additional for topping
8-10 pieces bacon, cooked and crumbled
12 eggs
12 C muffin tin

Preheat oven to 425°F. Grease the muffin tin cups. Mix hash browns, salt, pepper, oil and   C shredded cheese. Divide the mixture equally into the muffin tin. Bake hash browns for 15-18 minutes until toasty. When finished, remove from oven and lower the temperature to 350°F. Crack an egg into each of the cups, sprinkle with bacon and cheese. Bake 13-16 minutes, until eggs are done to your liking. Slide a knife along the edges to remove from pan when cooled. ◉

Egg Skillet

MEAGHAN SHAFFER
whatisarutabaga.com

4 eggs
1 medium sweet potato, shredded
1 C spinach
1 leek
2 Tbsp butter
Salt and pepper to taste

Preheat oven to 400°F. Melt 1 Tbsp butter in an oven-safe skillet. Add shredded sweet potatoes and cook until they begin to soften, 10-12 minutes. Add the remainder of the butter and the leeks and cook for another 5-7 minutes. Add the spinach and cook until just wilted. Create a little divot in four sections and crack eggs in each. Salt and pepper each egg. Transfer the skillet into oven and cook until the whites of the eggs are firm, about 12 minutes (less for more runny yolks). ◉

Crème Brulee French Toast with Drunken Strawberries

JAN BLOMEFIELD

½ C unsalted butter
1 C brown sugar, packed
2 Tbsp corn syrup
1 loaf challah or brioche bread, sliced into 1½-inch thick slices
5 large eggs
¾ C heavy cream
¾ C milk
1 tsp vanilla
¼ tsp salt
2 tsp Grand Marnier® or Cointreau®
Powdered sugar (optional)

Butter a 9x13 baking dish. In a small pot, melt the butter with the brown sugar and corn syrup. Stir together until the sugar is completely melted. Pour mixture into the baking dish. Place the bread slices on top of the butter and sugar mixture in one even layer. In a bowl, whisk together the eggs, cream, milk, vanilla, salt, and 2 tsp of Grand Marnier. Pour this mixture over the bread. Tightly cover baking dish with plastic wrap and refrigerate for 8 hours or overnight. Let dish stand at room temperature for 20 minutes before placing in preheated oven at 350°F. Bake 30-40 minutes until French toast is golden and puffed. Serve hot with drunken strawberries and optional powdered sugar sprinkled on top.

Drunken Strawberries
1 quart strawberries, hulled and sliced lengthwise, ¼-inch thick
¼ C sugar
¼ C Grand Marnier or Cointreau

Combine sliced strawberries, sugar, and Grand Marnier in a small bowl. Cover with plastic wrap and refrigerate for 2 hours, up to 24 hours.

Chili Egg Puff

CLARK BURTON

10 eggs, beaten or 16 oz egg beaters
½ C flour
1 tsp baking powder
½ tsp salt
16 oz carton small curd cottage cheese
16 oz Monterey Jack cheese, shredded
½ C margarine, melted
2-4 oz cans green chili peppers, drained and chopped

Preheat oven to 350°F. Combine first 7 ingredients, beating until blended. Add chili peppers. Pour into 9x13 glass baking dish. Bake 35 minutes or until brown and firm. Serves 12.

Caramel French Toast

EVE HARDIN

1 C brown sugar, packed
½ C butter
2 Tbsp light corn syrup
12 slices bread
6 eggs, beaten
1½ C milk
1 tsp vanilla
¼ tsp salt
1 C fresh raspberries

Combine sugar, butter, and corn syrup. Cook over medium heat until thick. Pour into 9x13 pan. Place 6 slices of bread on top, and place raspberries in center of bread. Place remaining 6 slices on top. Mix eggs, milk, vanilla, and salt until blended. Pour over the top, cover and chill overnight. Bake uncovered at 350° F for 40-45 minutes, until top is light brown. Place butter in center of each piece of toast and sprinkle powdered sugar. ◎

Brunch Egg Casserole

SARAH DENEAU

¼ C butter
4-6 oz mushrooms, chopped
2 bunches green onion
2 lbs hot sausage, cooked, crumbled, and drained
12 eggs
½ C cream
2 C shredded cheddar
2 C shredded Jack cheese
1 tsp salt
¼ tsp pepper
Red pepper (optional)

Sauté onion, mushrooms, and other veggies as desired in butter until tender. Add sausage and cook through. Beat eggs, cream, salt, and pepper. Add salt, optional pepper, cheese, and sausage mixture. Stir well. Pour into 9x13 baking dish. Bake about 60 minutes until set and golden brown. ◎

Martha's Favorite Granola

MARTHA ADAMSON

4-6 C uncooked, old-fashioned oatmeal
1½ C raw or toasted wheat germ
1 C grated coconut
¼ C powdered milk
2 Tbsp cinnamon
½ C sunflower and/or sesame seeds
½ C whole or chopped or sliced raw nuts, almonds, pecans, walnuts, pine nuts or any combination
1 Tbsp brown sugar
⅓ C vegetable oil
½ C honey
1 Tbsp vanilla
½ C dried fruit, raisins, cherries, blueberries, cranberries, or any combination

In a large bowl, combine the oatmeal, wheat germ, coconut, powdered milk, cinnamon, sesame seeds and nuts. Mix well. In a small saucepan, heat the brown sugar, oil, and honey until it just simmers, then remove from heat and add the vanilla. Stir until mixed. Add this to the dry mixture and stir until all is well coated. Spread mixture in a greased 9x13 baking pan or large rimmed baking sheet. Bake at 250° F for 60 minutes or 300° F for 30 minutes stirring the mixture at least once or twice to bake evenly. Remove from oven when nicely toasted. Cool in the pan, then add dried fruits, mixing well. Store in an air-tight container. Eat cold with milk, sprinkle on yogurt, or heat with milk and serve warm.

Guaranteed to make you happy and regular! ⊚

Slow Cooker Oatmeal (Diabetic Friendly)

SUE WILLIAMS

2 apples (2½-3 C chopped), peeled, cored, cut into ½-inch pieces
1 C fat-free milk or non-diary alternative such as almond milk
1½ C water
1 C uncooked steel-cut oats
2 packets Stevia® or 2 tsp agave
½ C unsweetened applesauce
½ tsp cinnamon
1 Tbsp ground flax seed
1 Tbsp whole flax seed
1 Tbsp chia seeds
¼ tsp salt
Optional garnishes: chopped dried cranberries, chopped nuts, raisins, maple syrup, additional ff milk or butter

Peel and chop apples. Spray inside of crock-pot with non-stick cooking spray. Add all ingredients, cover, cook on low 7-8 hours. Enjoy in the morning. Scoop into bowl, and add extra cinnamon to taste. You can also make this fresh in the morning on the stovetop. It takes approximately 45 minutes to cook. ⊚

Blueberry Coffeecake

BRIAN DENEAU

½ C brown sugar
½ tsp cinnamon
12 oz can refrigerated buttermilk biscuits
½ C butter, melted
1 C quick cooking oats
1½ C blueberries, fresh or frozen
½ C sugar

Preheat oven to 375°F. Grease 9x9 dish. Combine brown sugar and cinnamon. Cut biscuits into quarters. Dip biscuit in butter, coat with brown sugar mixture. Arrange in single layer in baking dish. Sprinkle with ½ C oats. Combine blueberries and sugar. Spoon over oats, then top with the rest of the oats. Drizzle remaining butter. Bake 20 minutes until golden brown and center is done. Cool 20 minutes and serve warm.

Egg Bake

LISA CAMPBELL

½ box seasoned Brownberry® croutons
½ box buttered Brownberry® croutons
½ lb Velveeta®, diced
8 eggs
4 C milk
1 tsp salt
8-10 strips bacon, cooked and crumbled

Preheat oven to 350°F. Grease 9x13 dish. Spread croutons on bottom of 9x13 glass pan. Place diced Velveeta on top of croutons. Beat 8 eggs, 1 quart milk (4 C), and 1 tsp salt together. Pour over croutons and cheese. Refrigerate overnight. Remove from refrigerator about 10 minutes before baking. Fry 8-10 strips of bacon. Crumble over the top. Bake 45-60 minutes or until eggs are slightly brown.

Crab Quiche

AIMEE DEARSLEY

2 Tbsp minced shallots
3 Tbsp butter
¼ lb (1 C) cooked crab or cooked shrimp or cooked lobster, diced
¼ tsp salt
Pinch pepper
2 Tbsp Madeira cooking wine
3 eggs
1 C whipping cream
1 Tbsp tomato paste
¼ tsp salt
Pinch pepper
8-inch partially baked pastry shell
¼ C grated Swiss cheese

Preheat oven to 375°F. Cook shallots in butter for 1-2 minutes over moderate heat until tender, but not browned. Add shellfish and stir gently for 2 minutes. Sprinkle salt and pepper. Add wine. Raise heat and boil for moment. Allow to cool slightly. Beat eggs in bowl with cream, tomato paste, and seasonings. Gradually blend in shellfish and taste for seasoning. Pour mixture into pastry shell and sprinkle the cheese over it. Bake at upper third of preheated oven for 25-30 minutes until quiche has puffed and browned.

Appetizers, Snacks, and Beverages

Baked Crab Rangoon

KATHLEEN KAMINSKY

⅛ tsp garlic salt
⅛ tsp Worcestershire sauce
1 small green onion, diced
4 oz imitation crab
3 oz cream cheese, softened
14 wonton wrappers

Preheat oven to 425°F. Microwave cream cheese for about 40 seconds to soften. Cut up crab and mix it in with garlic salt, Worcestershire sauce, diced green onion, and cream cheese. Spoon into wontons and seal the sides. Bake 8-10 minutes or until golden brown. ◉

Spiced Snack Crackers

LEE BREER

2 (12 oz) bags or boxes oyster crackers
1 C vegetable oil
1 package Hidden Valley® ranch dressing mix
1 Tbsp dry dill
1 tsp garlic powder
1 tsp Parmesan cheese

Place crackers into a plastic bowl with a tightly fitting lid. Place oil into a small bowl and add all the other dry ingredients. Mix well. Pour over the crackers and stir until well coated. Let stand for 24 hours. ◉

Dill Dip
GLORIA DAVIS

1 quart mayonnaise
1 pint sour cream
2 Tbsp parsley flakes
2 Tbsp onion flakes
2 tsp dill weed

Combine all ingredients. Refrigerate. Best if sits overnight.

Red and Green Pepper Jelly
ANNE MOORE

1 C red bell pepper, chopped
½ C jalapeño pepper, chopped
5 C white sugar
1½ C apple cider vinegar
6 oz liquid pectin

Remove stems and veins of pepper and mince in food processor. In 5-quart pot, on high heat, add peppers, sugar, and vinegar. Bring to rolling boil. Boil 3 minutes, remove from heat, and let cool for 5 minutes. Stirring continuously, add pectin and let cool for 2 more minutes. Stir 1 more minute. Pour into hot, sterilized jars and top with sterilized lids. Secure lids and allow to cool slowly to seal. Makes 6 (½-pint) jars. To double, use 10-12 jalapeños, 4-5 peppers, and 1 bag of sugar.

Bacon-Wrapped Water Chestnuts
LEE BREER

1 C catsup
1 C brown sugar
1 tsp Worcestershire sauce
16 oz sliced bacon
2 (8 oz) cans water chestnuts, drained

Preheat oven to 350°F. In saucepan, combine catsup, brown sugar, and Worcestershire sauce. Heat to boiling. Pour sauce over bacon and water chestnuts. Cut bacon slices into thirds. Cut larger water chestnuts in half. Wrap chestnuts in bacon and secure with toothpicks. Place in a 9x13 pan. Bake until bacon is completely cooked, 40-45 minutes.

Festival Tortillas

LEE BREER

2 (8 oz) packages cream cheese, softened
16 oz jar of your favorite salsa
1 envelope of Hidden Valley Festive Ranch® dressing mix
¼ C finely chopped black olives
1½ C shredded cheddar cheese
12-inch flour tortillas

Combine cream cheese, salsa, dressing mix, olives, and cheese. Spread on 12-inch tortillas and roll. Refrigerate all day or overnight. Cut into 2-inch pieces.

Apache Cheese Dip

MARY WHITEAKER

1 (9-inch) round loaf Hawaiian® bread
16 oz cheddar cheese
8 oz cream cheese, softened
8 oz sour cream
½ C minced green onions
1 tsp Worcestershire
2 (14.5 oz) cans chopped green chilies
1 C chopped ham

Cut and reserve top of bread. Scoop out inside of bread, leaving about 1 inch of crust all the way around. Combine ingredients. Bake uncovered in corning ware dish for 45 minutes. Spoon into bread bowl and replace top. Bake on cookie sheet for an additional 25 minutes. Remove top. Serve with chips or crackers.

Peach Mango Pineapple White Sangria

SARAH DENEAU

1 bottle white wine (Chardonnay, Pinot Grigio, Sauvignon Blanc, or similar)
⅓ C peach schnapps
¼ C sugar, or to taste (or Stevia®, agave, or another sweetener)
¾ C mango chunks, frozen
¾ C pineapple chunks, canned
⅓ C pineapple juice*
*use whatever is in the can

Combine first 3 ingredients in a large pitcher and stir until sugar dissolves. Add the remaining ingredients, stir, and refrigerate until chilled. Sangria can be stored for up to one week. Double, triple, or quadruple the recipe for a crowd. Sangria gets better 8-24 hours later. You should make this a day ahead if time and planning permits.

Pizza Snacks

TAM STONE

1 lb ground beef
½ lb hot pork sausage
2 lbs Velveeta® cheese, cut up
2 tsp oregano
1 package sliced or shredded mozzarella
3 loaves small party rye or 2 loaves square party rye

Preheat oven to 400°F. Cook meat and pour off grease. Add Velveeta and melt in the meat mixture. Add oregano and spread on party rye. Sprinkle with shredded mozzarella or cover with sliced mozzarella. Bake 10-12 minutes. Can also freeze ahead of time and bake just before serving. To freeze, place them on a cookie sheet. Once frozen, package in aluminum foil.

St. Joe's Church Funeral Luncheon Meatballs

MARGIE REDENBAUGH

5 lbs frozen meatballs
1 (12 oz) jar of chili sauce
12 oz water
14 oz sauerkraut, drained
16 oz whole can of cranberries
1 C brown sugar

Place all in crock-pot and let it cook until done.

Holiday Champagne Punch

TAM STONE

1 C triple sec
1 C brandy
½ C Chambord®
2 C unsweetened pineapple juice
1 quart ginger ale, chilled
2 (750 ml) bottles dry Champagne, chilled

In a covered bowl, combine triple sec, brandy, Chambord, and pineapple juice. Cover and chill for at least 4 hours or overnight. In a large punch bowl, combine triple sec mixture, ginger ale, and Champagne. Add ice cubes. Serves 16.

Tropical Drink

BARBARA SMOLINSKI

2 C fresh pineapple chunks
1 large banana
¾ C light coconut milk
¼-2 C agave nectar

Puree in blender and freeze in cubes. Enjoy.

Taco Dip

DONNA MALSON

2 (16 oz) cans Old El Paso® refried beans
1 lb cooked hamburger (chopped pieces)
8 oz sour cream mixed with 1 envelope of taco seasoning
12 oz Dean's® guacamole dip
7 green onions, finely chopped
1 (16 oz) can black olives, finely chopped
2 tomatoes, seeds spooned out and finely chopped
12 oz shredded cheddar cheese

Use a 13x9 dish or pan. Bake uncovered at 350°F for 20 minutes and serve with taco chips.

Hot Apple Pie Dip

PAM HAUK

8 oz cream cheese (⅓ less fat)
2 Tbsp brown sugar
½ tsp pumpkin pie spice
1 apple, chopped, divided
¼ C shredded cheddar cheese (2%)
1 Tbsp pecans (optional)
Wheat Thin® crackers

Preheat oven to 375°F. Mix cream cheese, sugar, and pie spice in bowl until well-blended. Stir in half of the apples. Spread into pie plate. Top with remaining apples, cheddar cheese, and optional nuts. Bake 10-12 minutes. Serve with crackers. Double this recipe for a large crowd. ⊚

Dirty Nachos

APRIL CAYCE

1 lb ground beef
2½ C water
2 Tbsp vegetable oil (optional)
1 package Zatarain's® dirty rice mix, original
1 bag Tostitos® scoop chips
1 jar Tostitos® queso cheese

In large skillet, brown ground beef on medium-high heat in optional vegetable oil. Drain fat. Set aside. Bring water to boil in medium saucepan. Stir in rice mix and ground beef; return to boil. Reduce heat to low; cover and simmer 25 minutes or until rice is tender. Remove from heat. Let stand 5 minutes. Fluff with fork before serving. Place as many scoops on plate as you can fit. Sprinkle dirty race on top of nachos to your satisfaction. Pour queso cheese on top. ⊚

Marmalade Fruit Dip

AVIS AYERS

8 oz cream cheese, softened
8 oz sour cream
⅓ C orange marmalade
2 Tbsp brown sugar

Mix together, chill. Serve with assorted fruit.

Sausage Balls

AVIS AYERS

1 lb uncooked ground sausage
3 C Bisquick®
8 oz Cheese Whiz®
½ C milk

Preheat oven to 400°F. Mix together well. Form into 1-inch balls. Bake 10-15 minutes on an ungreased baking sheet.

Jalapeño Popper Dip

SARAH DENEAU

2 (8 oz) packages cream cheese, room temperature
1 C mayonnaise
1 C shredded Mexican blend cheese
½ C grated Parmesan
1 (4 oz) can green chilies
1 (4 oz) can jalapeños or 4 fresh seeded jalapeños, diced finely (add more if you like it hotter)
1 C panko breadcrumbs
½ C grated Parmesan cheese
¼ C butter, melted

Preheat oven to 375°F. Mix the first 6 ingredients together and spread the dip into a greased pie pan or a 2-quart baking dish. In a bowl, mix panko breadcrumbs, remaining ½ C Parmesan cheese, and melted butter until incorporated. Sprinkle crumb mixture evenly over the dip and bake about 20 minutes or until top is browned and the dip is bubbly. Serve with chips, crackers, or baguette slices.

Mexi Corn Dip

ANGELA SCHRIEWER

1 C sour cream
2 (11 oz) cans Mexi corn
3 green onions, chopped
Pinch of cumin
Salt
Pepper
1 jalapeño, diced
1 C mayonnaise
1 can green chilies
8 oz shredded Mexican cheese

Mix all ingredients in bowl and chill overnight. Serve with tortilla chips. ◉

Pumpkin Dip

AVIS AYERS

16 oz can pumpkin pie mix (not pumpkin)
2 (8 oz) packages cream cheese
2 lbs confectioners' sugar

Mix cream cheese and pumpkin pie mix, add confectioners' sugar. Chill. Serve with ginger snaps, sliced apples, sugar cookies. ◉

Buffalo Chicken Dip

CHARLES GLEASON

1 (8 oz) package cream cheese
½ C ranch or blue cheese dressing
¾ C Franks Red Hot® sauce
2 C shredded cheese
2 (12.5 oz) cans white, breast meat chicken

Drain the chicken thoroughly and mash it up in a mixing bowl. A good, sturdy fork works well for this. Soften the cream cheese for 30-45 seconds in the microwave and combine it with the chicken. Mix in the ranch dressing, hot sauce, and shredded cheese of your choice. Combine thoroughly and transfer to a 9x9 pan. Bake at 350°F for 20 minutes. Serve warm with tortilla chips.

Alternatives: Substitute 2 medium-sized breasts, cooked to your liking, and shredded with a grater. Refrigerate breasts for at least 30 minutes before grating. Combine half Pepper Jack and half Mexican cheese for added kick– and adjust hot sauce to taste. Enjoy!

Pineapple Dip

SANDY BOURNE

12 oz jar pineapple preserves
12 oz jar apple jelly
¼ C dry mustard
¼ tsp ground horseradish
8 oz cream cheese

Mix preserves, jelly, mustard, and horseradish together. Pour over block of cream cheese and serve with crackers.

Finger Sandwiches

DAWN HARROD

1 (8oz) package cream cheese, softened
Dash of Tabasco
1 medium cucumber, peeled and chopped finely
1 small onion
Dash of salt and pepper
1 small package party rye bread

Combine first 5 ingredients and spread on party rye bread. Serve chilled.

Mom Kersten's Cream Cheese Dip

LISA CAMPBELL'S GREAT GRANDMA

8 oz Philadelphia® cream cheese and 1 or more Tbsp milk needed to soften
1 Tbsp mayonnaise
4 Tbsp sour cream
1 tsp Worcestershire sauce
1 tsp celery salt
1 tsp onion salt
1 tsp garlic powder or more to taste

Soften cream cheese. Add all seasonings and sour cream. Add more sour cream if preferred. Serve with chips, pretzels, or corn chips. ◉

Red Sangria

AIMEE DEARSLEY

¼ C sugar
2 (750 milliliter) bottles dry red wine (Columbia Crest Two Vines® Merlot recommended)
½ C orange juice
*½ C peach nectar*or additional ½ C orange juice*
¼ C orange liqueur (Grand Marnier® recommended)
2-3 C club soda, chilled
1 lemon, thinly sliced
1 lime, thinly sliced
1 orange, thinly sliced
1 Granny Smith apple, thinly sliced
usually found in the international food aisle with the fruit juices or with cocktail mixes

Bring sugar and 1¼ C water to a boil in a saucepan over medium-high heat, stirring occasionally, until sugar is dissolved. Remove from heat, and let stand 10 minutes. Combine sugar mixture, red wine, and next 3 ingredients in a large container; cover and chill 4 hours. Stir in club soda and next 4 ingredients just before serving. Serve over ice, if desired.

Sangria Blanco
Omit orange juice and peach nectar. Substitute dry white wine for red wine, lemon-lime soft drink for club soda, and 1 pt fresh strawberries for 1 Granny Smith apple. Increase orange liqueur to 1 C, 1 lemon to 2, 1 lime to 2, and 1 orange to 2. Prepare recipe as directed, stirring in ¾ C loosely packed fresh mint leaves with wine in Step 2. ◉

Garlic Pecans

Jennifer Offt

1 lb pecans, halved
½ C salted butter, melted
¼ C Worcestershire sauce
2 Tbsp garlic powder
Salt to taste

Preheat oven to 275°F. Combine all ingredients in a large mixing bowl, stirring to coat the pecans evenly. Spread pecans onto a baking sheet and place in the middle rack of oven. Toss pecans every 15 minutes for a total of 45 minutes, watching carefully so as to not burn. Pour pecans back into a large bowl, sprinkle liberally with salt and enjoy!

Spinach Dip

NAN BENNETT AND JAN BALVEN

1 C Hellmann's® mayonnaise*
1 C sour cream
½ package Hidden Valley® ranch dressing mix
1 (10 oz) package spinach, thawed and drained

Combine all ingredients. Serve with tortilla chips or crackers.

*Must use Hellmann's brand mayonnaise.

MaiN DiSHeS

Fake White Castles

KAREN ZINKL-TAYLOR

1½ lbs ground beef
1 package dry onion soup mix
1 (11 oz) can mushroom soup
1 lb Velveeta® cheese
½ C butter
1 large onion, chopped

Brown onion in butter, and add ground beef. Brown ground beef. Place mixture into crock-pot. Cut up cheese and add to meat mixture. Mix dry soup and can of soup into crock-pot. Heat until cheese is melted, on high for approximately 60 minutes. Once melted, turn crock-pot on low or warm. Add a little more butter if mixture is too thick once cheese melts. Spread over buns. Pickles are optional, but they taste great with this.

Great for the crock-pot. I have doubled this recipe for parties! ◉

Lazy Person's Dinner

LINDA MACADAM

1-2 Tbsp olive oil
1 large potato, with skin
½ large onion
¼ lb ground round, veggie ground round, or ground chicken
Salt

Cut onion into bit-sized pieces and lightly brown in the olive oil. Wash and slice potato into ¼-inch thick slices, add to onions and brown. Place a lid on pan and turn heat to low. Cook for 20 minutes. Remove lid, add ground round, turn up heat and stir until ground round is cooked. Salt to taste. Serves 1.

Easy and delicious! ◉

Sweet Ham and Swiss Sliders

JOY WHITMAN

16 white dinner-style rolls, cut in half
24 slices honey ham
16 slices Swiss cheese
¼ C mayonnaise
1½ Tbsp Dijon mustard
8 Tbsp butter, melted
1 tsp onion powder
½ tsp Worcestershire sauce
1 Tbsp poppy seeds
¼ C brown sugar

Preheat oven to 400°F. On a rimmed baking sheet place bottom half of dinner rolls and top with 1½ slices of ham and 1 slice Swiss cheese. Spread about 1 tsp of mayonnaise on each top half of roll and place on top of ham and cheese. The rolls should be snug in the pan, touching enough so the sauce can soak into all of the nooks and crannies. In a small bowl combine the mustard, melted butter, onion powder, Worcestershire sauce, poppy seeds, and brown sugar. Mix until combined and evenly pour over the assembled rolls. Cover with foil and refrigerate until ready to bake. Bake covered with foil for 10 minutes, remove the foil and bake an additional 5-10 minutes or until tops are browned, and cheese is good and melted. ◎

Baked Chicken Legs

KELLY GIESLER

12 chicken legs
Milk, enough to cover chicken
½ Tbsp parsley
Salt and pepper to taste
⅓ C Parmesan cheese
½ C bread crumbs

Soak 12 chicken legs in milk for 30 minutes. Mix all other ingredients in large bowl and cover each leg with the mixture. Place on a baking sheet, sprayed with non-stick cooking spray. Cook for 50 minutes at 400°F. For crispness, spray the chicken lightly with non-stick cooking spray. 260 calories per serving. ◎

Mexican Jambalaya

NANCY MIRIANI

1 (8 oz) sour cream
1 (16 oz) large jar salsa
1 medium red onion, chopped or frozen chopped onion
2 (15 oz) cans red beans of any kind, with liquid
2 C white rice, cooked
1 (15 oz) can of chopped Mexican-style tomatoes or 1 carton of small tomatoes, chopped
1 envelope taco seasoning
1 clove garlic, chopped
1 (16 oz) Mexican-style Velveeta® cheese
1 container Old El Paso®, or comparable brand, shredded chicken or beef

Place everything in a crock-pot and cook on low for a couple of hours, or on high for 60 minutes, until ingredients are cooked and melted. Add water for desired consistency, if needed. Serve with tortillas or chips. 🌀

Stephanie's Chicken

STEPHANIE WEAVER

4-6 boneless, skinless chicken breasts
4-6 slices Provolone cheese, cut in half
Baby spinach leaves
Roma tomatoes, sliced ¼-inch thick

Preheat oven to 350°F. Clean any fat from the chicken breasts. Place in bowl and add enough olive oil to lightly coat the chicken breasts. Toss them or use tongs to slide around until thoroughly coated.

Place large skillet on medium-high heat. When hot, add chicken breasts and turn heat down to medium. Cook for a couple minutes to get a nice sear on the chicken. Turn over and cook the other side.

Use non-stick cooking spray to lightly grease a baking dish large enough to hold all of the chicken without crowding (9x13 for 6 chicken breasts). Bake 30 minutes. Remove chicken. Set oven to broil. While it heats, place 2-4 baby spinach leaves on top of each chicken breast to cover, placed end-to-end. Place 3 slices of tomato on top of each breast. Top each breast with one slice of cheese, overlapping the halves so they do not hang down onto pan. Broil in oven until cheese bubbles and browns to your taste. 🌀

Baked Spaghetti

MELISSA OBERNUEFEMANN

1 C chopped white onion
1 C chopped green pepper
1 (14-16oz) can Rotel® chopped tomatoes and green chilies
1 (4 oz) can mushrooms
1 (2½ oz) can sliced black olives
2 tsp oregano
2 tsp garlic salt
1 lb ground chuck
12 oz cooked spaghetti
¼ C water
2 C shredded cheddar
1 can cream of mushroom soup
Parmesan cheese

Cook ground chuck, onion, and pepper in skillet. Drain. Add tomatoes/chilies, mushroom, olives, oregano, and garlic salt. Simmer uncovered for 10 minutes. Place half of cooked noodles into greased 13x9 dish. Top with half of meat mixture. Sprinkle with 1 C cheddar and amount of Parmesan to your liking. Repeat layer. Mix soup with water and pour over casserole and smooth over top. Sprinkle with Parmesan. Bake at 350°F, 30-40 minutes, uncovered. ◉

Allyson's Enchilada Casserole

ALLYSON RYAN

4-5 flour tortillas, torn in pieces
1 (11 oz) can cream of chicken soup
1 (28 oz) large can enchilada sauce
2 C cooked chicken torn into pieces
2 C shredded cheese (2% Mexican blend recommended)
1 (15 oz) can black beans, rinsed

Preheat oven to 350°F. Mix soup, enchilada sauce, and ½ can of water in bowl. Add black beans.

Spray 9x13 baking dish with non-stick cooking spray. Spread 5-6 Tbsp of soup mixture in bottom of dish, enough to coat the dish. Place torn tortilla pieces in dish. Layer chicken, soup mixture, and cheese. Then repeat layers of tortilla pieces, chicken, soup mixture, and cheese. Top with remaining cheese. Bake 25-30 minutes until bubbly around the edges. Cover with foil if it gets too brown. ◉

Tacos

MEAGHAN SHAFFER

whatisarutabaga.com

1 lb ground beef
2 bell peppers, sliced
1 medium yellow onion, sliced
1 Tbsp chili powder
1½ tsp cumin
1 tsp salt
1 tsp pepper
½ tsp paprika
¼ tsp garlic powder
¼ tsp crushed red pepper
¼ tsp oregano
3 Tbsp extra virgin olive oil

Mix all seasonings (everything but the meat, onions, peppers, and oil) in a small bowl. Set aside. Heat olive oil in a frying pan over medium to medium-high heat. Add onions to pan and cook, 5-7 minutes. Add peppers to the pan, cook for about 5 minutes. Add ⅓ of the seasoning mix and coat the onions and peppers. Cook until peppers have softened. Add beef and the rest of the seasoning, stirring and coating well. Cook until the beef is completely done, no pink. Serve over flour or corn tortillas. ⊚

Chicken and Dumplings

ALLYSON RYAN

2 (11 oz) cans cream of chicken soup
1 (11 oz) can cream of mushroom soup
3 cans water
2 cans refrigerated biscuits*
2 C cooked chicken torn into pieces (grocery store rotisserie chicken recommended)
*use two of the smaller cans that are sold in a package of four cans

Bring all liquids to a slight bubbling boil. Roll biscuits out flat. Place pieces of cooked chicken on biscuit and wrap tightly. Drop into boiling broth. Boil uncovered 10 minutes. Cover and cook 10-20 minutes more, until done. Dumplings will float to surface as they cook. ⊚

American Lasagna

MOLLY MOHRMAN

1 lb lean ground beef
1 lb Italian sausage
1 onion, chopped
2 cloves garlic, minced
1 Tbsp chopped fresh basil
1 tsp dried oregano
2 Tbsp brown sugar
1½ tsp salt
1 (28 oz) can diced tomatoes
2 (6 oz) cans tomato paste
12 lasagna noodles, cooked
2 eggs, beaten
1 (16 oz) pint ricotta cheese
½ C grated Parmesan cheese
2 Tbsp dried parsley
1 tsp salt
1 lb shredded mozzarella cheese or mozzarella/Provolone blend
2 Tbsp grated Parmesan cheese

Preheat oven to 375°F. In a skillet over medium heat, brown meat, onion, and garlic; drain fat. Mix in basil, oregano, brown sugar, 1½ tsp salt, diced tomatoes, and tomato paste. Simmer 30-45 minutes, stirring occasionally. In a medium bowl, mix together eggs, ricotta, Parmesan cheese, parsley and 1 tsp salt. Layer ⅓ of the cooked lasagna noodles in the bottom of a 9x13 baking dish. Cover noodles with half of the ricotta mixture, half of the mozzarella cheese, and a third of the sauce. Repeat. Top with remaining noodles and sauce. Sprinkle additional Parmesan cheese over the top. Bake 30-40 minutes. Let stand 10 minutes before serving. If prepared the day before and refrigerated, bake 50-60 minutes and let stand for 10 minutes before serving. ◉

Beef with Noodles

SANDY BOURNE

2 lbs stew beef or other cut of lean beef
1 package dry onion soup mix
1 (11 oz) can condensed cream of mushroom soup
1 can 7-up® soda
Cornstarch to thicken
Cooked noodles or rice

Add all ingredients in a crock-pot and cook on low for 6-8 hours. When finished, add cornstarch to thicken gravy. Serve over noodles or rice. ◉

Derrick's Baked Ziti

KERRI AULABAUGH

1 lb meat (hamburger and venison recommended, but omit if desired)
36 oz spaghetti sauce
1 (15 oz) container of ricotta cheese
1 egg
1 C sour cream
1 lb mozzarella
¼ C Parmesan

Preheat oven to 360°F. Cook ziti 8-10 minutes. Drain and rinse. Mix ricotta, egg, 2-3 C sauce, most of mozzarella, and sour cream. Add to ziti. Spread sauce in bottom of a square pan or 11x13 pan. Fill pan with ziti and cheese mixture. Cover with remaining sauce, half of the mozzarella, then Parmesan. Place remaining mozzarella on top. Bake 30 minutes. Let stand 15 minutes. ◉

Mostaccioli Recipe

SARAH DENEAU

1 lb ground beef
1 lb ground sweet Italian sausage
1 onion
2 cloves garlic
1 tsp pepper
1 tsp Italian Seasoning (Penzey's® recommended)
1 Tbsp sugar
1 tsp salt
2 bay leaves
6 oz tomato paste
1 (26 oz) jar spaghetti sauce
1 can cheddar cheese soup
4 C mozzarella, divided
16 oz box mostaccioli

Preheat oven to 350°F. In a Dutch oven, boil the noodles, drain when done and set aside. In the Dutch oven heat a little olive oil, cook the meat with the onions and garlic. When the meat is browned, add the seasonings, tomato paste, sauce, soup, and 2 C mozzarella. Mix well. Place in oven for 20 minutes until cheese is melted. Top with 2 C mozzarella and serve. ◉

Bob's Sweet and Sour Meatloaf

BOB BELL

1 (8 oz) can tomato sauce
¼ C brown sugar
¼ C vinegar
1 tsp mustard
2 lbs ground beef
1 C sliced mushrooms
1 egg, slightly beaten
¼ C onion, diced
¾ C crackers or bread
1 tsp salt
¼ tsp pepper

Preheat oven to 400°F. Combine tomato sauce, brown sugar, vinegar, and mustard into a bowl making sure all ingredients are dissolved. Set aside. Combine ground beef, mushrooms, egg, onion, bread/crackers, salt, and pepper. Pour in half of the tomato sauce/brown sugar mixture. Knead all ingredients until sauce is mixed in thoroughly with the rest of the ingredients. Place mixture into a regular meatloaf pan and pour the other half of sauce over the meatloaf as a cover. Bake 45 minutes or until meat is completely done. Serves 4-5.

Chicken Casserole

BILLIE MIERS

1 (11 oz) can cream of mushroom soup
1 soup can of milk (more or less for moisture)
2 Tbsp mayonnaise
½ C shredded cheddar cheese
5 slices American cheese
1 small onion, diced
¼ each red, green, yellow pepper, diced (optional)
1 stalk celery, diced
Salt, pepper, Original Mrs. Dash® to taste
2 C chicken,*baked and cubed
½ box mostaccioli or penne noodles
¼ C bread crumbs or cracker crumbs moistened with butter

*2 cans of tuna can be substituted for tuna casserole

Mix first 9 ingredients in a saucepan and heat over medium heat until cheese is melted. Add chicken and mix well. Cook noodles al dente. Slowly add sauce mixture to cooked noodles and stir gently. Mixture should be fairly moist. Pour into a casserole dish prepared with non-stick cooking spray. Top with bread crumbs and bake uncovered at 400°F for 20-30 minutes or until sauce is bubbling and bread crumbs are golden brown. Cool at least 10-15 minutes before serving.

Tamale Pie

BILLIE MIERS

1 lb ground chuck*
1 lb ground sausage*
1 pack taco seasoning
1 (11 oz) can whole kernel corn
1 (15 oz) can black beans
1 can sliced black olives (optional)
1 (4 oz) small can green chilies, chopped (optional)
1 (28 oz) can or jar enchilada sauce
½ pint sour cream
2 C shredded cheese, cheddar or Mexican blend
12 oz jar salsa
2 packages Betty Crocker® cornbread mix, prepared to cook**
*cooked and cubed chicken can be used in place of ground chuck and ground sausage
**add extra milk to make pouring and spreading easier

Cook ground chuck and sausage in taco seasoning according to directions. Layer all ingredients, except cornbread, in order in a large baking dish. Prepare a thin layer of prepared cornbread mix and pour over the top. Bake until the cornbread is brown and the mixture is bubbling. Cool at least 15 minutes before serving. Turn individual servings upside down and top with additional shredded cheese and/or sour cream. ◎

Marinated Barbequed Pork Chops

JOHN JACKSON

4 pork loin butterfly chops
½ C LaChoy® soy sauce
½ C French's® Worcestershire sauce
½ C red wine vinegar
Adolph's® meat tenderizer
Onion powder
Garlic salt
Poultry seasoning

Rinse pork chops with cold water, making sure all bone fragments are removed. Treat pork chops with Adolph's meat tenderizer following the directions on the container. Rub pork chops with onion powder, garlic salt, and poultry seasoning to taste. Place pork chops flat in a 1-gallon food storage bag. Mix soy sauce, Worcestershire sauce, and red wine vinegar in a medium-sized bowl. Pour marinade into the food storage bag and seal the bag. Let pork chops soak in marinade overnight in the refrigerator. Turn the bag over at least once to ensure pork chops absorb the marinade evenly. Barbeque pork chops until well done on a charcoal or gas-fired grill. ◎

Salmon with Creamy Dill Sauce

KATHY HOPPE

1 salmon fillet, about 2 lbs
1-1½ tsp lemon-pepper seasoning
1 tsp onion salt
1 small onion, sliced and separated into rings
6 lemon slices
¼ C butter, cubed

Dill Sauce
⅓ C sour cream
⅓ C mayonnaise
1 Tbsp finely chopped onion
1 tsp lemon juice
1 tsp prepared horseradish
¾ tsp dill weed
¼ tsp garlic salt
Pepper to taste

Line a 15x10x1 baking pan with heavy-duty foil; grease lightly. Place salmon skin-side down on foil. Sprinkle with lemon-pepper and onion salt. Top with onion and lemon. Dot with butter. Fold foil around salmon; seal tightly. Bake at 350°F for 20 minutes. Open foil carefully, allowing steam to escape. Broil 4-6-inches from the heat for 8-12 minutes or until the fish flakes easily with a fork. Combine the sauce ingredients until smooth. Serve with salmon. Serves 6. ◎

Crock-pot Shredded Chicken Tacos

ANGELA SCHRIEWER

1 (3 lb) package frozen, boneless, skinless chicken breasts
1 (16 oz) jar salsa
1 package taco seasoning
Hard taco shells or tortillas
Fixings for tacos (lettuce, tomatoes, cheese, sour cream, etc.)

Place salsa and taco seasoning into crock-pot. Mix together. Add frozen chicken. Cover and cook on high 4-6 hours or on low 6-8 hours. Shred chicken. Arrange tacos.

Alternatives: Some people place the chicken back into the crock-pot before adding to tacos. If you are out of shells, you can have this with lettuce on a plate. Place lettuce down, then meat and toppings.

My kids don't like the chunks that salsa has so we don't "reuse" it on our tacos. ◎

Roast with Pepsi Gravy

KAREN S. FREEBERSYSER

1 (3-4 lb) beef roast
1 (11 oz) can cream of mushroom soup
1 package dry onion soup mix
1 (16 oz) regular Pepsi®, not diet

Place all ingredients in roaster and cover tightly. Bake at 350°F for 3-4 hours. The roast will make its own gravy, so have a pot of mashed potatoes ready to go.

Easy Pleasing Meatloaf

PAM HAUK

2 lbs lean ground beef
1 C water
1 (6oz) package Stove Top® stuffing mix for chicken
2 eggs, beaten
½ C BBQ sauce, divided (Sweet Baby Ray's® recommended)
Onions (optional)

Preheat oven to 375°F. Mix all ingredients except for ¼ C BBQ sauce. Place in 13x9 baking dish; top with remaining BBQ sauce. Bake 60 minutes or until done (160°F).

Beth's Beer BBQ Chicken

BETH ZIMMER

2-4 skinless boneless chicken breasts
Olive oil
1 small onion, diced
1 (12 oz) bottle of beer
½ beer bottle of water
1 bottle of BBQ sauce

Sear chicken in 2 Tbsp extra virgin olive oil on high heat. Cook 5-7 minutes until brown on both sides. Chop 1 small onion and throw in skillet. Add more olive oil to cover bottom of pan. Cook onion down until almost brown. Add one bottle of beer. Refill with ½ bottle of water. Bring to boil, boil down 5-10 minutes. Empty most of liquid, but not onions. Add bottle of BBQ sauce. Cook on low for 30 minutes or longer.

Homemade Stuffed Crust Pizza

PEGGY BURGESS

Sauce
1 (6 oz) can tomatoes
2 (6 oz) cans tomato paste
½ C dry red wine
4 tsp instant minced onions
1 tsp basil
1 tsp oregano
1 tsp parsley flakes
½ tsp garlic salt

Pizza
Dough for 2 crusts
3 lbs shredded mozzarella cheese
20 oz Italian sausage
Parmesan cheese (optional)

Mix sauce ingredients and bring to boil, simmer 10 minutes. Shape sausage into marble-sized balls and brown. Place one crust on bottom of pan and press it up sides. Sprinkle cheese on bottom and alternate sausage and cheese in layers. Place second crust over top and seal both crusts. Bake at 425°F for approximately 20 minutes. Pour sauce on top of crust and place back in oven for approximately 15 minutes.

Mom said sprinkling Parmesan cheese over the sauce maintains the moisture.

Chinese Five Spice Beef Tournedos

TAM STONE

1½ lbs beef tenderloin
Chinese five spice
Kosher salt
¼ C olive oil

Cut tenderloin into 2-3 oz medallions. Coat medallions with olive oil. Season with Chinese five spice and kosher salt to taste. Heat pan on medium-high heat and coat with olive oil. Sear medallions until desired doneness.

Rocky Mountain Brisket with Barbecue Sauce

PEGGY BURGESS

Brisket
1½ tsp salt
1½ tsp pepper
2 Tbsp chili powder
1 tsp crushed bay leaves
2 Tbsp liquid smoke
4 lbs beef brisket

Combine salt, pepper, chili powder and bay leaves. Rub meat completely with liquid smoke. Place meat, fat side up, in a large roasting pan. Sprinkle dry seasoning mixture on top. Cover tightly, bake 4 hours at 325°F. Scrape seasoning off meat and cut in very thin slices across the grain. Serve with BBQ sauce.

Sauce
3 Tbsp brown sugar
1 (14 oz) bottle catsup
½ C water
2 Tbsp liquid smoke
4 Tbsp Worcestershire sauce
3 tsp dry mustard
2 tsp celery seed
6 Tbsp butter
¼ tsp cayenne pepper

Combine all ingredients. Bring to a boil, stirring occasionally. Cook 10 minutes. Slice brisket and place in sauce to serve. Place in a crock-pot to keep warm.

Chicken and Rice

KATHY MICELLI

4 boneless, skinless chicken breasts
1 (11 oz) can cream of mushroom soup
1 (11 oz) can cream of celery soup
1 (11 oz) can cream of chicken soup
1 C rice
Salt and pepper to taste

Combine soups and rice and mix well. Add salt and pepper. Lay chicken on top. Bake at 350°F and turn once, until chicken is done, depending on the thickness of the chicken breasts, 35-40 minutes. Stir well.

Smoked Macaroni and Cheese with Fire Roasted Tomatoes

NANCY WELLER

3 C uncooked elbow macaroni
1½ C whipping cream
1 tsp Dijon mustard
½ tsp coarse kosher or sea salt
¼ tsp ground red cayenne pepper*
12 oz smoked cheddar cheese, shredded**
2 (14.5 oz) cans Muir Glen® organic, fire roasted, diced tomatoes, drained well
½ C sliced green onions
⅓ C grated Parmesan cheese**
⅓ C plain dry bread crumbs
2 tsp olive oil
*this makes a world of difference in the taste
**shredded, not the powdery kind

Preheat oven to 375°F. Cook and drain macaroni as directed on box. Return to saucepan; cover to keep warm. Spray 13x9 glass baking dish with non-stick cooking spray. In 2-quart saucepan, heat whipping cream, mustard, salt, and red pepper to boiling. Reduce heat; stir in cheddar cheese with wire whisk until smooth. Pour sauce over macaroni. Stir in tomatoes and onions. Pour into baking dish. In small bowl, mix Parmesan cheese and bread crumbs. Stir in oil. Sprinkle over top of macaroni mixture. Bake uncovered 15-20 minutes or until edges are bubbly and top is golden brown.

Smoked cheddar cheese and Muir Glen fire roasted tomatoes are the secret ingredients that give this updated mac 'n cheese its intense flavor. ◎

Spicy Chicken Fettuccine

KAREN S. FREEBERSYSER

¼ C butter or margarine
½ C onion, diced
1 garlic clove, minced
1 (4 oz) can mushrooms, drained
1 (11 oz) can cream of chicken soup
1 soup can filled with milk
1 lb Mexican Velveeta® cheese, cubed
1 lb fettuccine noodles, cooked
2 C cooked chicken
1 (10 oz) package frozen peas, broken apart

Preheat oven to 350°F. Sauté onion, garlic, and mushrooms in butter or margarine until tender. Mix with soup, milk, and cubed cheese. Prepare fettuccine noodles according to the package. Place cooked fettuccine in greased 9x13 baking dish. Top with chicken, peas, and soup mix. Bake 30 minutes. ◎

Stuffed Pork Tenderloin

SANDY BOURNE

1 pork tenderloin, butterflied, and pounded to about ¼-inch thickness
Olive oil
1 medium apple, chopped
½ large onion, chopped
½ C breadcrumbs
Fresh spinach
Provolone cheese, sliced
Salt, pepper, garlic powder to taste

Preheat oven to 350°F. Sauté apple and onion in olive oil until tender. Mix in breadcrumbs. Top pork with spinach leaves and Provolone. Spread with apple, onion, and breadcrumb mixture. Roll the tenderloin tightly and secure with toothpicks. Bake 30-45 minutes until done. ☺

Chicken Tostadas

MICHELLE STREIFF

1 onion, chopped
1 Tbsp oil
1 jalapeño, finely chopped
1 tsp salt
8 oz tomato sauce
2 C chicken, cooked and shredded or chopped (grilling with Mexican spice rub recommended)
Guacamole
Sour cream
Tostada shells

Grill chicken or buy already cooked chicken breast. Let cool and shred or chop. Cook onion in oil until just browned, stir in jalapeño, salt, and tomato sauce. Simmer covered 5 minutes. Stir in chicken and heat through. Prepare guacamole (mash avocado with salt, pepper, garlic, oregano, and lemon juice) or use store-bought. Bake tostada shells as directed, pile on chicken mixture and guacamole. Top with sour cream. ☺

Mexican Lasagna

MARY WHITEAKER

1 lb ground beef
1 onion, chopped
1 (10 oz) can Rotel® tomatoes and chilies
1 (8 oz) can tomato sauce
½ tsp cumin
1 tsp salt
½ tsp pepper
4 oz cream cheese, softened
½ C sour cream
12 oz shredded Colby-Monterey Jack cheese
3 (10-inch) large flour tortillas

Preheat oven to 350°F. Spray 9-inch square casserole dish with non-stick cooking spray. Brown ground beef with onion and drain. Add Rotel, tomato sauce, cumin, salt, and pepper and simmer for 15 minutes. In a separate bowl, mix together cream cheese and sour cream. Layer as follows: place one tortilla in casserole dish. Cover with half the cream mixture. Top with half the beef mixture. Sprinkle with a third of the cheese. Repeat with another layer of the above, then cover with the third tortilla and the remaining shredded cheese. Bake 30 minutes. Serve with garnishments of tomatoes, diced green onions, shredded lettuce, olives, and sour cream. ◎

Chicken Puffs

ANGELA SCHRIEWER

8 oz cream cheese, softened
1 (12.5 oz) can of chicken
¾ C grated onion
2 Tbsp butter, melted
2 oz sherry or white wine
3 (8-count) packages crescent rolls

Preheat oven to 375°F. Mix together cream cheese, onion, sherry, chicken and melted butter. Cut each crescent roll in half. Spread dough out with fingers and Place a spoonful of mixture in the middle. Fold up by bringing each corner to the middle. Bake 20 minutes. ◎

Red Beans and Rice

NANCY WELLER

1 lb dry red beans
1 lb Andouille or other spicy sausage
1 large onion, chopped
1 green pepper, chopped
½ C chopped celery (optional)
2 cloves minced garlic
8 C water or chicken broth
2 bay leaves
1 Tbsp Worcestershire sauce
2 tsp Creole Seasoning
Dash hot sauce
Salt and pepper

In large bowl, soak beans in hot water and cover for at least 60 minutes. Drain and set aside. In large pot, cook sausage until done and sauté onions, green pepper, garlic and optional celery until tender. Add beans, water, and remaining ingredients. Bring to boil, reduce heat and cover for 30 minutes. Remove cover and simmer on low at least 2 hours until beans are tender. Mash a quarter of the mixture against the side of the pot to thicken and stir. Remove bay leaf and serve over cooked rice with salad and French bread.

Creole Seasoning
2½ Tbsp paprika
2 Tbsp salt
2 Tbsp garlic powder
1 Tbsp freshly ground pepper
1 Tbsp onion powder
1 Tbsp cayenne
1 Tbsp dried oregano
1 Tbsp dried thyme 🌀

Aglio Olio (Garlic and Olive Oil Pasta)

SHAWNA DAVINROY

1 lb cooked angel hair pasta, drained but not rinsed
½ C olive oil
6-8 cloves garlic, peeled and minced finely
½ tsp dried red pepper flakes
Salt and pepper to taste
¼ C chopped fresh parsley or fresh basil
½ C Parmesan cheese

Boil pasta per instructions. Sautee garlic and dried red pepper flakes in about 1 tsp of olive oil for approximately 30 seconds (garlic burns easily). Mix together all remaining ingredients with pasta while still hot.

Poppy Seed Chicken

SARAH DENEAU

2 sleeves Ritz® crackers, crumbled
1 C butter, melted
3 Tbsp poppy seeds
3-4 large boneless chicken breasts, cooked and cut up
2 (11 oz) cans cream of chicken soup
8 oz sour cream

Preheat oven to 325°F. Mix crackers, melted butter, and poppy seeds together, Set aside. Layer ¾ of the cracker mixture on bottom of 9x13 pan. Top with cut up chicken. Mix soup with sour cream. Cover the chicken. Top with remaining cracker crumbs. Bake about 45 minutes.

Uncle Don's Salmon Croquettes

DONALD CHARTRAND

1 (15 oz) can pink salmon, skin and bones removed
1 egg, slightly beaten
2½ Tbsp Worcestershire sauce
½ tsp salt
½ C bread crumbs
2 Tbsp chopped onion
2 Tbsp margarine

Thoroughly mix above items. Shape mixture into 4 pear-shaped units. Place croquettes on a cookie sheet. Preheat oven to 350°F. Bake 20 minutes. Top with creamed peas for a delicious meal. ☺

Spaghetti with Pecorino Romano and Black Pepper (Cacio E Pepe)

PAT CZOSNYKA

6 oz Pecorino Romano cheese (4 oz finely grated and 2 oz coarsely grated)
1 lb spaghetti
Table salt
2 Tbsp heavy cream
2 tsp extra-virgin olive oil
1½ tsp finely ground black pepper

Place finely grated Pecorino in medium bowl. Set colander in large bowl. Bring 2 quarts water to boil in large Dutch oven. Add pasta and 1½ tsp salt; cook, stirring frequently, until al dente. Drain pasta into colander/bowl, reserving cooking water. Pour 1½ C cooking water into liquid measuring cup and discard remainder; return pasta to now-empty bowl. Slowly whisk 1 C reserved pasta cooking water into finely grated Pecorino until smooth. Whisk in cream, oil, and black pepper. Gradually pour cheese mixture over pasta, tossing to coat. Let pasta rest 1-2 minutes, tossing frequently. Adjust consistency with remaining ½ C reserved pasta water. Serve, passing coarsely grated pecorino separately. ☺

Roasted Chicken and Spicy Peanut Soba Noodles

PAT CZOSNYKA

½ C toasted sesame oil
4 garlic cloves, minced
1 Tbsp minced fresh ginger
2 Tbsp Sriracha hot sauce
3 Tbsp honey
½ C creamy peanut butter
2 Tbsp lemon juice
¼ C low-sodium soy sauce
¼ C hot water
4 C shredded chicken from a whole roasted deli-chicken
½ lb dried buckwheat soba noodles

In a small sauté pan heat sesame oil. Add garlic and ginger to gently fry until fragrant—about 1 minute. Pour into a blender and add hot sauce, honey, peanut butter, lemon juice, soy sauce, and hot water. Blend until smooth, adding more hot water if necessary to achieve a rich saucy consistency. Cook soba noodles according to packet directions, then drain and pour into a large mixing bowl. Add 4 C shredded chicken meat and dress with spicy peanut sauce. Use tongs to work sauce into chicken and noodles gently. Top with green salad (see below).

Green Salad
½ hothouse cucumber, thinly sliced
3 ribs of celery, thinly sliced on the bias
1 C cilantro leaves
2-3 scallions, finely sliced on the bias

In a small mixing bowl combine cucumber, cilantro, and scallions. Toss gently to combine. Divide noodle mix evenly among bowls and top with a handful of green salad. ◉

Argentinean Pork

ELAINE SMITH

6 Tbsp olive oil, divided
1 C fresh parsley leaves, divided
⅔ C fresh cilantro leaves, divided
½ tsp ground cumin
¼ tsp crushed red pepper
1 (1-lb) pork tenderloin, trimmed
¾ tsp kosher salt, divided
½ tsp black pepper
Non-stick cooking spray
1 Tbsp fresh oregano leaves
1 Tbsp fresh lemon juice
1 Tbsp sherry vinegar
2 garlic cloves, chopped
1 shallot, chopped

Combine 2 Tbsp oil, ¼ C parsley, ⅓ C cilantro, cumin, and red pepper in a shallow dish. Add pork. Cover with plastic wrap, and refrigerate 60 minutes, turning once. Preheat grill to medium-high. Sprinkle pork with ½ tsp salt and black pepper. Place pork on a grill rack coated with cooking spray, and grill for 8 minutes. Turn pork over, and grill 7 minutes or until a thermometer registers 145°F. Remove pork from grill. Let stand for 5 minutes. Slice pork crosswise.

Sauce
Combine ¾ C parsley, ⅓ C cilantro, ¼ tsp salt, oregano, and remaining ingredients in a food processor; pulse 10 times. Drizzle ¼ C olive oil through food chute with food processor on. Serve with pork.

Sticky Orange Chicken

SANDY BOURNE

2 Tbsp extra virgin olive oil
1 whole chicken, cut into pieces
½ C white wine
Salt and pepper
½ C chicken stock
¼ C orange marmalade
2 lemons, 1 sliced into rings, 1 zested and juiced

Preheat oven to 350°F. Place large skillet on medium heat with oil. Season chicken with salt and pepper and sear until golden brown, about 4 minutes per side. Transfer to an ovenproof dish, and finish cooking, about 20 minutes. Deglaze the skillet with white wine, then add chicken stock, marmalade, and lemons. Reduce heat to medium-low and cook until sauce is thickened. Pour over chicken.

Barbequed Dry-Rubbed Chicken

ELAINE SMITH

3 Tbsp dark brown sugar, packed
2 tsp chili powder
2 tsp paprika
1½ tsp pepper
1 tsp dry mustard
1 tsp onion powder
1 tsp salt
¼ tsp cayenne pepper
3 lbs bone-in chicken pieces (cut breasts in half), trimmed

Combine all ingredients except chicken in a bowl. Set aside half of mixture in a shallow bowl. Pat chicken dry and coat over and under skin with remaining rub. Cover and refrigerate for 30-60 minutes. For a charcoal grill, open the bottom vent completely, and pour lit coals over whole grill bottom. Open the lid vent completely and heat the grill until hot, about 5 minutes. For gas, turn all burners to high, cover, heat until hot, then turn burners to medium-low. Arrange the chicken pieces skin side down. Grill until the skin is well browned and crisp, 15-20 minutes. Lightly dredge the skin side of the chicken with reserved rub and return it to the grill, skin side up. Grill, covered, until the rub has melted into a glaze and the chicken is fully cooked, 15-20 minutes longer. Breasts should register 160°F; thighs and drumsticks 175°F. Transfer chicken to a plate, tent with foil, and let rest 5 minutes.

Chicken with Artichokes and Olives

AIMEE DEARSLEY

2 C sliced fresh mushrooms
1 (14.5 oz) can tomatoes
1 (8-9 oz) package frozen artichoke hearts
1 C chicken broth
1 medium onion, chopped
½ C sliced, pitted ripe olives or ¼ C capers, drained
¼ C dry white wine or chicken broth
3 Tbsp quick cooking tapioca
2-3 tsp curry powder
¾ tsp dried thyme, crushed
¼ tsp salt
¼ tsp pepper
1½ lbs skinless, boneless chicken breast halves and/or thighs
4 C hot cooked couscous

In a 3½-4-quart slow cooker, combine the mushrooms, undrained tomatoes, frozen artichoke hearts, chicken broth, onion, olives or capers, and wine or broth. Stir in tapioca, curry powder, thyme, salt, and pepper. Add chicken; spoon some of the tomato mixture over the chicken. Cover; cook on low heat for 7-8 hours or on high heat setting for 3½-4 hours. Serve with hot cooked couscous.

Rich 'n Cheesy Baked Macaroni

GINNY ENDEJEAN

2½ C uncooked big elbow pasta (rigati preferred)
6 Tbsp butter, divided (unsalted preferred)
1-2 cloves garlic, minced
¼ C flour
1 tsp salt, decrease slightly
1 tsp sugar
Pinch cayenne pepper (smoky chipotle recommended)
½ tsp seasoned or regular pepper, decrease slightly
Pinch grated nutmeg
2 C whole or 2% milk
8 oz Velveeta®, cubed
1⅓ C regular small-curd cottage cheese
⅔ C sour cream
8 oz shredded sharp cheddar cheese
1½ C soft sourdough bread crumbs

Cook pasta according to package directions until al dente; drain. Place in buttered 3-quart baking dish. This will easily fit in a 13x9 pan. If a smaller dish is used, place on a foil-covered sheet pan to catch drips. In a saucepan, melt 4 Tbsp butter. Add minced garlic and cook until fragrant, about 30 seconds. Stir in flour, salt, sugar, cayenne, pepper, and nutmeg until smooth. Gradually stir in milk. Bring to a boil; cook and stir for 2 minutes or until thickened. Reduce heat; stir in Velveeta until melted. Stir in cottage cheese and sour cream. Pour over pasta. Sprinkle with cheddar cheese. Melt remaining butter and toss with bread crumbs; sprinkle over top (entire surface or just perimeter of dish). Bake uncovered, 350°F for 30 minutes or until golden brown.

Burrito-In-A-Bowl

GINNY ENDEJEAN

1 large onion, largely dice
3-4 cloves garlic, chopped
1 tsp hot chili powder
4 C cooked brown rice
1 recipe Cook's Foolproof Brown Rice®, cooked with broth/salt
2 C salsa
1½ tsp cumin
1 tsp chili powder
15 oz can fat-free, refried beans
10 oz frozen corn kernels, thawed
4 oz can chopped green chilies
2 Tbsp Chili Con Carne powder
10 oz frozen chopped spinach, thawed and squeezed
3 oz reduced-fat cheddar cheese
2 Tbsp fat-free sour cream (per serving)
⅓ small can sliced black olives (per serving)
Aleppo pepper for serving

Preheat oven to 375°F. Spray a small non-stick skillet with cooking spray. Sauté onion, garlic, and 1 tsp hot chili powder until onion is translucent. Set aside. In a large bowl, combine brown rice, salsa, cumin, and 1 tsp chili powder; mix well. In a medium bowl, combine refried beans, reserved onion mixture, corn, green chilies, and 2 Tbsp chili powder; mix well. In a 2-quart casserole sprayed with non-stick cooking spray, spoon half of the rice mixture; spread to cover bottom of dish. Scrape bean mixture on top of rice layer and smooth out. Spread spinach on top of bean layer; top with the cheese. Spoon remaining rice mixture on top and smooth out. Cover with non-stick foil and bake 30 minutes. Top each serving with sour cream and black olives.

6 Weight Watchers points. ◉

Bowtie Pasta

LISA AND JACK BERGFELD

3 Tbsp butter
8 oz fresh mushrooms, sliced
6-8 oz dried tomatoes
1 bunch of asparagus, top portion cut into 2-inch pieces
½ medium-sized zucchini, sliced
½ medium-sized yellow squash, sliced
1 Tbsp slivered garlic
1¼ C chicken broth
1¼ C whipping cream
½ C dry white wine
12 oz bowtie or penne pasta
3 Tbsp fresh herbs (basil, parsley, chives, tarragon, or combination)
Spritz of lemon juice
⅔ C freshly grated Parmesan cheese
Salt and pepper

Boil water for pasta. Perform all cutting and slicing. After adding pasta to boiling water, start the sauce. In a large skillet, melt butter. Add mushrooms, zucchini, and garlic. Cook over medium-high heat until vegetables just begin to color. Add broth, cream, asparagus, squash, wine, and tomatoes. Stir occasionally until sauce reduces slightly, about 4 minutes. Pasta should be firm to the bite (al dente). Drain and add directly to the skillet. Stir in herbs, half the cheese, and a spritz of lemon. Add salt and pepper to taste. Coat all of the noodles with the sauce. Serve with additional Parmesan cheese on top and garlic bread on the side. ⟲

Creamy Garlic Pasta

MELANIE LEHR

2 tsp olive oil
4 cloves garlic, minced
2 Tbsp butter
¼ tsp salt
½ tsp pepper
3 C chicken stock
½ lb spaghetti or angel hair pasta
1 C grated Parmesan cheese
¾ C heavy cream
2 Tbsp chopped fresh parsley

In a pot, bring the olive oil to medium-low heat. Add the garlic and stir, allowing it to cook for 1-2 minutes. Mix in the butter until melted. Add the salt, pepper, and chicken stock. Raise the heat to high and let it come to a boil. Once it is at a rolling boil, add the pasta and cook according to package directions. Reduce the stove to medium heat and mix in the Parmesan until completely melted. Turn off the heat and stir in the cream and parsley. Serve immediately. ⟲

SOUPS AND SALADS

Rebecca's Black Bean Salad

CHRISTINA M. ERSKINE

2 (15 oz) cans black beans, rinsed and drained
11 oz can whole kernel corn, drained or 2 C thawed frozen corn
½ C low-fat mayonnaise
½ C green pepper strips
½ C sliced red onion
2 Tbsp chopped fresh cilantro or more to taste
2 Tbsp lime juice
1 garlic clove, minced
½ tsp ground cumin
½ tsp salt
¼ tsp ground red pepper

Mix all ingredients in large bowl; refrigerate several hours or overnight. ◎

Cream Cheese Potato Soup

DONNA MCCALL

6 C chicken broth
6 C potatoes, peeled and cubed
½ C onions, minced
1 tsp salt (more or less as desired)
¼ tsp white pepper
¼ tsp ground red pepper
2 carrots, thinly sliced
1 (8 oz) package cream cheese

Combine broth, potatoes, onion, and spices. Boil on medium heat until potatoes are tender. Smash a few of the potatoes to release their starch for thickening. Reduce to low heat. Add thin sliced carrots, cook 10 minutes. Add cream cheese. Heat, stirring frequently, until cheese melts. ◎

Taco Bean Soup

SALLIE CORTELYOU

1 (15 oz) can black beans with liquid
1 (15 oz) can pinto beans with liquid
1 (15 oz) can northern beans with liquid
1 (15 oz) can garbanzo beans with liquid
1 (28 oz) can crushed tomatoes
1 (8 oz) can, diced green chilies
½ envelope taco seasoning mix
1 envelope ranch salad dressing mix
3 shakes garlic powder and onion powder

Add all ingredients to crock-pot. Cook on low until heated through, 4-8 hours. This soup is very forgiving, so if you need to cook it longer it's ok. Serve with tortilla chips, grated cheese, sour cream and/or salsa. ◎

Aunt Jan's Beer Cheese Soup

BRIAN DENEAU

¼ C butter or margarine
½ C flour
⅔ C milk
1 (13¾ oz) can chicken broth
1 (8 oz) jar of Cheez Whiz®
¼ C beer
½ tsp Worcestershire sauce

Melt butter, stir in flour until smooth. Add milk and chicken broth in gradual amounts stirring until smooth. Heat until bubbly and thickened. Reduce heat, add Cheez Whiz, and stir until melted. Simmer 5-10 minutes, stirring occasionally. Add beer and Worcestershire sauce, heat but do not boil. ◎

Caramel Apple Salad

MOLLY MOHRMAN

6 Granny Smith apples
5 regular-sized Snickers® bars
16 oz container whipped topping
1 small can crushed pineapple

Chop candy bars into ¼-inch pieces. Core and dice apples into ½-inch pieces, including the skin. Mix together with pineapple and whipped topping. Core and cut 2 apples at a time, place in bowl, and drizzle some pineapple/ juice over as you go to keep the apples from turning brown. Refrigerate candy bars for a couple of hours before chopping to keep them from sticking to the knife. For added color, use one Red Delicious apple. Improvise to make a larger or smaller batch. Use fun size candy bars if preferred.

DJ's Grandma's Coleslaw

JOY WHITMAN

1 large head of cabbage, chopped
½ C onion, chopped
½ C sliced carrots
½ C oil
¾ C vinegar
1 Tbsp sugar
1 Tbsp salt
⅛ tsp pepper
1 tsp celery seed
½ tsp dry mustard

Place first 4 ingredients in a bowl and pour 1 C sugar over the cabbage and let stand for 30 minutes. Boil together ½ C oil, ¾ C vinegar, 1 Tbsp sugar, 1 Tbsp salt, tsp pepper, 1 tsp celery seed, and ½ tsp dry mustard. Pour over cabbage and let sit covered overnight in the refrigerator. Mix and enjoy.

Macaroni Salad

KAREN BRADBURY

1 lb macaroni
1 (14 oz) can Eagle Brand® condensed milk
2 C real mayonnaise
1 C sugar
¾ C white vinegar
1 small or medium red onion
1 green pepper
Celery seed to taste

Cook macaroni to package directions. When cool, add all other ingredients. Sprinkle with celery seed. ☺

Mini Caprese Bites

MICHELLE STREIFF

1 pint grape or cherry tomatoes
10-14 small fresh mozzarella cheese balls, cut into thirds
32 (4-inch) wooden skewers
¼ C extra virgin olive oil
2 Tbsp balsamic vinegar
¼ tsp kosher salt
¼ tsp pepper
6 fresh basil leaves, thinly sliced
Kosher salt and pepper to taste

Thread 1 tomato half, 1 piece of cheese, and another tomato half onto each skewer. Place skewers in a shallow serving dish or individual serving dishes. Whisk together oil and next 3 ingredients. Drizzle oil mixture over skewers; sprinkle with basil, salt and pepper to taste. Use marinated mozzarella on your favorite salad and skip the dressing! ☺

Roquefort Dressing

TAM STONE

1 lb bleu (Roquefort) cheese
1 medium onion, finely chopped
2 hard-boiled eggs, finely chopped
2 C mayonnaise
1 oz brandy or cognac
Salt and pepper to taste
Cream

Combine all ingredients except cream. Beat well by hand. Add cream to desired thickness. Makes 1 quart.

Spicy Sweet Potato Bisque

TERYN GILMORE

2 large sweet potatoes or yams, peeled and cubed
1 Tbsp olive oil
1 onion, sliced
2 cloves garlic, sliced
4 C vegetable or chicken broth
½ tsp cumin
¼ tsp red pepper flakes
2 Tbsp fresh grated ginger
¼ C peanut butter (optional)

In stock pot, heat olive oil. Add onion and garlic and sauté until onion is softened, about 5 minutes. Add sweet potatoes, vegetable stock, cumin, pepper flakes, and ginger. Bring to a boil. Reduce heat to low and cover. Cook 20 minutes, or until the potatoes are soft. Puree soup in blender. Small batches work best. Return soup to pot. Add optional peanut butter. Heat through until peanut butter is melted. Enjoy!

Best Ever Chicken Tortilla Soup

KATHLEEN KAMINSKY

3 Tbsp olive oil
1½ (7-inch) corn tortillas, cut into 1-inch squares
1½ Tbsp minced fresh garlic
2 Tbsp minced white onion
1½ tsp minced jalapeño pepper
1 lb white corn kernels
1½ lbs ripe red tomato, chopped
⅓ C tomato paste
2½ tsp ground cumin
1 Tbsp kosher salt
⅛ tsp ground white pepper
½ tsp chili powder
1½ C water
1 quart chicken stock
24 blue corn tortilla chips (garnish)
2 C shredded cheddar cheese (garnish)
½ C chopped fresh cilantro (garnish)

Over medium-high heat, fry tortilla squares in olive oil until they begin to crisp and turn a golden yellow. Add garlic, onion, and jalapeño; cook 1-2 minutes until onion is translucent. Add half the corn along with all other ingredients (except garnishes), reserving other half of corn to be added at the end. Bring the soup to a low, even boil. Boil for 5 minutes. Remove soup from heat. Use a hand held blender to process in batches to the consistency of a coarse puree, or process in batches in a blender. Return the soup to the burner and add the reserved corn. Bring the soup to a boil once again, being extremely careful to avoid scorching or burning the soup. Serve, garnished with blue tortilla chips, cilantro, and cheddar cheese. ◉

Spaghetti Salad

KAREN BRADBURY

1 lb spaghetti
1 cucumber
1 green pepper
1 onion
2-3 tomatoes
Large bottle of Catalina dressing
Small bottle of Italian dressing
1 tsp Salad Supreme seasoning

Cook spaghetti, drain. Place half of everything in bowl, mix well. Pour remainder of everything in bowl and mix. Sprinkle Salad Supreme on top. ◉

Oriental Slaw

KAREN S. FREEBERSYSER

Slaw
1 medium head cabbage, chopped
½ C slivered almonds, toasted
4 green onions, chopped
½ C sesame seeds, toasted
2 packages of any flavor Ramen® oriental noodles

Crush noodles while still in package. Brown sesame seeds, slivered almonds, and noodles in 250°F oven for 15-20 minutes. Set aside. Combine cabbage and green onions in bowl, cover and refrigerate until ready for dressing.

Dressing
⅓ C artificial sweetener or ¼ C sugar
1 C salad oil (vegetable, canola, corn, peanut, or other light-flavored oil)
2 tsp salt
7 Tbsp rice vinegar or regular vinegar
1 tsp black pepper

Combine all ingredients in a jar and shake well. When ready to serve add sesame seeds, slivered almonds, and noodles to the cabbage and onion. Then pour dressing over and mix well. The dressing may be stored in the refrigerator until ready to use. Discard the seasoning packets from the Ramen oriental noodles. ◎

Aunt Brenda's Strawberry Salad

KATHRYN PARK

8 oz cream cheese, softened
¾ C sugar
12 oz strawberries
1 (20 oz) large can crushed pineapple, drained
2 bananas, sliced
1 C nuts
1 (8 oz) container whipped topping

Cream together cream cheese and ¾ C sugar. Add 12 oz strawberries, crushed pineapple, bananas, and nuts. Fold in carton whipped topping. Can be frozen. ◎

Crock-pot White Chicken Chili

ALICIA MINER

2 jars (3 lbs) of great northern white beans with liquid
4 lbs of chicken breast cooked and cubed
2 Tbsp olive oil
8 cloves of garlic
4 medium white onion
1 tsp ground cumin
¼ tsp ground cloves
2 tsp oregano
½ tsp cayenne pepper, or more to taste
4 (4 oz) cans mild chopped green chili
6 C chicken broth
16 oz Monterey Jack cheese
Sour cream
Sliced canned jalapeño

Cook chicken and cut into cubes. Heat oil, add onion, and cook until translucent. Stir in garlic, chilies, cumin, cayenne, oregano, cloves. Sauté for 2-3 minutes. In crock-pot, add chicken, onion mixture, beans, chicken broth, and 1 bag of Monterey Jack cheese. Cook on low 6-8 hours. Simmer on stovetop for about 60 minutes until all the spices have time to merge. Serve with sour cream, jalapeño, and top with 2-3 Tbsp of Monterey Jack cheese. Halve the ingredients for a smaller batch. ◎

Spicy Corn Chowder

NANCY WELLER

1 (4 oz) jar chopped pimento, drained
1½ C chopped onion
2 Tbsp butter or margarine
1 Tbsp flour
1 Tbsp chili powder
1 tsp ground cumin
1 (16 oz) package sweet corn
2 C salsa (mild recommended)
1½ C chicken broth
1 (8 oz) package cream cheese, softened
1 C milk

Sauté onions in butter in large pan, stir in flour and seasonings. Add corn, salsa, broth, and pimento and bring to a boil. Gradually add ¼ hot mixture to cream cheese in bowl, stirring until well-blended. Add back into pan with milk. Cook until thoroughly heated–do not boil. Add chopped cooked chicken or ham for a heartier dish. ◎

Mrs. O'Brien's Black Bean Soup

NANCY WELLER

1 lb bag black beans
2 Tbsp olive oil
1 whole tomato, slightly green
1 bay leaf
½ medium onion, whole
½ medium green pepper, whole
1 clove garlic, whole
1 tsp oregano
¼ tsp cumin
2 Tbsp wine vinegar
1 Tbsp salt
½ tsp hot sauce
Cooked rice

Soak beans overnight in water. The next day, drain and rinse beans. Place beans in a large pot and add enough water to cover by 1-inch. Add olive oil, tomato, bay leaf, onion, green pepper, and garlic. Let cook 60 minutes, stirring frequently. Remove tomato, bay leaf, onion, green pepper, and garlic and let simmer. In a frying pan sauté in olive oil, half onion, chopped, half green pepper, chopped, 1 clove garlic, minced until onion is limp. Add oregano, cumin, wine vinegar, salt, and ½ tsp hot sauce Cook for 2 minutes, then add to beans. Add more water if needed. Simmer for 60 minutes or longer. When ready to serve, place 1 heaping Tbsp of rice in a soup bowl then add soup. Serve with chopped onions and salad and bread. ◎

Strawberry Jello Salad

SANDY BOURNE

3 (3 oz) packages strawberry banana jello
2 C boiling water
Dash of salt
1 (20 oz) large can crushed pineapple, drained
30 oz frozen strawberries, chopped
2 C mashed bananas
16 oz sour cream

Dissolve jello and salt in boiling water in a large mixing bowl. Add pineapple, strawberries, and bananas to the jello mixture. Pour half of the mixture into a 9x13 pan and place in refrigerator until jelled. Spread sour cream onto jelled mixture and top with remaining jello. Place in refrigerator until well set. ◎

Sausage, Kale, and White Bean Soup

NANCY WELLER

1 C dry navy beans
1 C chopped shallots
4 C chicken broth
1 large bunch kale, rinsed, stemmed and chopped
1 Tbsp olive oil
1 lb spicy linguica sausage, sliced
Salt and pepper to taste
½ tsp hot sauce or to taste

Place the navy beans into a large container and cover with several inches of cool water; let stand 8 hours or overnight. Drain and rinse before using. Cook the soaked beans in a pressure cooker in 4 C water for 25 minutes. Use the natural release method to release pressure. Do not drain. Bring a separate pot of salted water to a boil. Add the kale and simmer until kale is bright green and tender, about 2 minutes. Drain in a strainer, and cool under cold running water. Set aside. Heat olive oil over medium heat in the soup pot. Brown the linguica slices on each side, about 5 minutes. Remove from the pot with a slotted spoon and set aside. Add shallots to pot and cook until soft, about 3 minutes. Pour in a splash of chicken broth and scrape up any browned bits of sausage. Return the sausage to the pot along with the beans and their cooking liquid. Stir in the chicken broth. Bring soup to a boil, reduce heat to low, and simmer uncovered for 15 minutes. Add the kale and cook about 4 minutes longer. Season with salt, pepper, and hot sauce to taste. ⊚

Pineapple Marshmallow Delight

KAREN S. FREEBERSYSER

2 (3 oz) packages lemon gelatin
2 C hot water
2 C cold water
1 (20 oz) can drained crushed pineapple
1 (6½ oz) package miniature marshmallows
½ C reserved pineapple juice
1 egg, beaten
½ C sugar
1 Tbsp flour
1 Tbsp melted butter or margarine
1 (8 oz) package cream cheese
1 (2 oz) envelope powdered whipped topping mix (Dream Whip®)
1 C chopped nuts

Dissolve gelatin in hot water, add cold water. Add pineapple and marshmallows to gelatin. Pour into 10x12x1½ utility dish. Chill until firm. Combine pineapple juice, egg, sugar, flour, and melted butter in a saucepan. Cook on medium heat until mixture thickens. Remove from heat; add cream cheese and beat until smooth. Cool. Prepare topping mix according to package directions. Fold into cheese mixture. Spread over firm gelatin layer. Sprinkle with nuts. Chill until firm. Serves 12-16.

Warm Chicken and Couscous Salad with Almonds

Kathryn Park

¼ C extra virgin olive oil
1 shallot, coarsely chopped
¾ C couscous
1 C chicken stock or broth
3-4 Tbsp dried currants or cranberries
3½ lbs roasted chicken, shredded
Sprinkle parsley
¼ C salted roasted almonds coarsely chopped
3 Tbsp lemon juice
Salt and freshly ground black pepper

In a small pan, heat 1 Tbsp oil. Add the shallot and cook over high heat until lightly browned, 1-2 minutes. Stir in couscous. Add the stock and currants and bring to a boil. Cover the pan, remove from the heat and let stand for 5 minutes. Fluff the couscous with a fork and transfer to a large bowl. Add the chicken, parsley, almonds, lemon juice and remaining 3 Tbsp olive oil. Season with salt and pepper and toss well.

Chicken Stew

NANCY WELLER

2 Tbsp olive oil
2 stalks celery, cut into bite-sized pieces
1 carrot, peeled, cut into bite-sized pieces
1 small onion, chopped
Salt and freshly ground black pepper
1 (14½ oz) can chopped tomatoes
1 (14 oz) can low-salt chicken broth
½ C fresh basil leaves, torn into pieces
1 Tbsp tomato paste
1 bay leaf
½ tsp dried thyme leaves
2 chicken breasts with ribs (about 1½ lbs total)
1 (15 oz) can organic kidney beans, drained and rinsed if not organic

Heat the oil in a heavy 5½-quart saucepan over medium heat. Add the celery, carrot, and onion. Sauté the vegetables until the onion is translucent, about 5 minutes. Season with salt and pepper to taste. Stir in the tomatoes with their juices, chicken broth, basil, tomato paste, bay leaf, and thyme. Add the chicken breasts; press to submerge. Bring the cooking liquid to a simmer. Reduce the heat to medium-low and simmer gently uncovered until the chicken is almost cooked through, turning the chicken breasts over and stirring the mixture occasionally, about 25 minutes. Transfer the chicken breasts to a work surface and cool for 5 minutes. Discard the bay leaf. Add the kidney beans to the pot and simmer until the liquid has reduced into a stew consistency, about 10 minutes. Discard the skin and bones from the chicken breasts. Shred or cut the chicken into bite-sized pieces. Return the chicken meat to the stew. Bring the stew just to a simmer. Season with salt and pepper to taste. Ladle the stew into serving bowls and serve with crusty bread.

Bean Soup

PAT STRUCKEL

Ham bone
3 stalks celery, chopped
1 large onion chopped
2-3 carrots, chopped
2 (15 oz) cans of great northern beans with liquid
1 (15 oz) can great northern beans, mashed
6-8 (15 oz) cans great northern beans, drained
1-2 cans potatoes, drained
Pepper to taste

Place ham bone in large pot, cover with water and simmer until meat falls off the bone (3+ hours). During the last 15 minutes, add carrots, all great northern beans. Simmer 30 minutes. Check for consistency. Add potatoes. Add pepper to taste.

Strawberry Pretzel Jello Salad

SARAH DENEAU

3 C crushed pretzels
3 Tbsp sugar
¾ C melted butter
6 oz box regular strawberry jello
2 C boiling water
16 oz frozen strawberries
8 oz crushed pineapple, drained
8 oz whipped topping
8 oz cream cheese
1 C sugar

Preheat oven to 400°F. For crust, stir pretzels, 3 Tbsp sugar, and melted butter together. Pour into 9x13 pan and pack it down. Bake 7 minutes. Allow to cool. In bowl, stir jello into boiling water. Dissolve. Cool jello. Thaw strawberries and drain pineapple. Stir fruit into jello. Cream together the sugar and cream cheese. Add whipped topping until mixed. Spread cream cheese mixture over crust. Pour jello on top of cheese layer. Refrigerate for several hours. ◉

Fresh Tomato Soup

KAREN S. FREEBERSYSER

5 large tomatoes
1 small onion, halved and thinly sliced
1 bay leaf
¼ tsp garlic powder
½ tsp seasoned salt, without MSG
½ tsp cilantro
¼ tsp thyme
½ tsp chicken bouillon
1 tsp sugar
½ tsp pepper
¼ tsp Cavendar's® Greek seasoning mix
½ C milk
4 Tbsp butter
8 oz Kraft® processed cheese
2 Tbsp cornstarch dissolved in ½ C water

Peel and quarter tomatoes. Cook tomatoes, onion, and next 9 spices in 2 C water for 30 minutes. Remove bay leaf. Mash tomatoes with a potato masher. Add milk and butter. Heat until melted. Add cheese a little at a time until melted. Mix cornstarch with water and add to soup until desired consistency. ◉

Cashew Pear Salad

SARAH DENEAU

Salad

1 bunch of Romaine
1 C shredded Swiss cheese
1 C cashews
1 medium pear, thinly sliced
1 medium apple, any kind, thinly sliced
½ C craisins
4 oz goat cheese

Dressing

⅔ C olive oil
½ C sugar
1 tsp Dijon mustard
⅓ C lemon juice
3 tsp poppy seeds
2 tsp finely chopped green onion
1 tsp yellow mustard
½ tsp salt

Toss salad ingredients together in large bowl. Blend dressing ingredients together and mix well. Pour over salad ingredients and toss to coat. Serve immediately. ◎

Homemade Chicken Soup

KAREN S. FREEBERSYSER

5 lbs stewing chicken cut into pieces (do not skin)
1 medium onion, diced
3 carrots, chopped
4-5 stalks of celery, chopped
5 whole clove spice
2 bay leaves
Water to cover chicken
Salt and pepper to taste
1 package egg noodles
1 can whole potatoes (optional)

Combine all ingredients in a stock pot. Bring to a boil. Skim top of soup as it is cooking. Simmer until chicken is tender about 60-75 minutes. Remove chicken and shred. Return shredded chicken to stock pot. While soup is simmering, prepare egg noodles according to package. Drain egg noodles. Place egg noodles in individual bowls. Ladle soup over noodles. Warm optional whole potatoes in small pot and add 1 or 2 to bowl of soup. ◎

No Peak Stew

KAREN S. FREEBERSYSER

2½ lbs stew meat (not browned)
4 potatoes, peeled and chopped
4 carrots, peeled and chopped
4 stalks celery, chopped
3 small onions, diced
1¼ C tomato juice (Campbell's® recommended)
3 Tbsp tapioca
1 Tbsp sugar
1 (28 oz) large can whole tomatoes
Salt to taste
Black pepper to taste

Cut up meat and vegetables and place in large roasting pan. Add other ingredients and mix together. Bake covered at 350°F for 5 hours without uncovering.

The above is for a regular-sized batch stew. Increase the amount of meat and chopped vegetables and use the entire can of tomato juice for more leftovers. The recipe is "No Peek," but a peek after 3 hours is ok, especially with the increased ingredients. 🌀

Southwest White Chili

BRIAN HOELTGE

1 Tbsp olive oil
3 lbs boneless, skinless chicken breast, cut into small cubes
2 tsp onion powder
3 (14 oz) cans chicken broth
2 (4 oz) cans chopped green chilies
4 cans white kidney beans
Southwest Spice Blend

Southwest Spice Blend
Mix 2 tsp garlic powder, 2 tsp ground cumin, 1 tsp oregano leaves, 1 tsp cilantro leaves, and ¼ tsp ground red pepper all together until well-blended.

Heat oil in large saucepan over medium-high heat. Add chicken and onion powder. Cook until all chicken is white. In large stock pot, combine chicken broth, green chilies, Southwest Spice Blend, and chicken. Simmer 25-30 minutes. Add beans. Cook another 5 minutes. Garnish with Monterey Jack cheese, if desired. 🌀

Black Bean, Corn, and Tomato Salad

PAT CZOSNYKA

4 ears corn-on-the-cob
2 Tbsp red wine vinegar
2 cloves garlic, minced
⅛ tsp salt
Ground pepper to taste
5 Tbsp olive oil
1 bunch cilantro
3 C cooked (1 C dried) black beans, rinsed and drained or 2 cans drained and rinsed
1 carton grape tomatoes
1 C red onion, chopped

Boil corn-on-the-cob until done, approximately 5 minutes. Allow to cool enough to handle, then remove kernels and set aside. In a small glass jar add together red wine vinegar, garlic, salt and ground black pepper and olive oil. Then shake. Toss with dressing in a serving bowl: black beans, corn, cilantro leaves, grape tomatoes, and red onions. Serve. ◉

Roasted Asparagus Soup

PAT CZOSNYKA

2 bunches green onions
1½ lbs asparagus, cut into 2-3-inch pieces
1 medium onion, cut into thin wedges
2 Tbsp olive oil
2 (14 oz) cans chicken broth
¼ tsp salt
¼ tsp freshly ground pepper
½ C half-and-half or ½ C light cream or ½ C milk
1 Tbsp snipped fresh dill
Fresh dill sprigs

Preheat oven to 450°F. Trim root ends from green onions. Cut white parts into 1-inch lengths. Cut green tops into 1-inch lengths and reserve. Place the white parts, asparagus, and onion wedges in an even layer in a shallow large roasting pan. Drizzle vegetables with olive oil. Roast, uncovered, for 15-20 minutes or until vegetables are charred and tender. Place half of the roasted vegetables in a food processor or blender. Add half of a can of broth. Cover; process or blend until smooth. Transfer to a large saucepan. Repeat with remaining asparagus, onion wedges, and half of a can broth. Stir in remaining can of broth, salt, and pepper. Heat through. Stir in half-and-half and snipped fresh dill. To serve, ladle soup into bowls. Top with reserved green sections of onion and dill sprigs. ◉

Quickie Brunswick Stew

CHRISTY DENEAU

1 (15 oz) can crushed tomatoes
2 (15 oz) cans creamed corn
1 (10 oz) can Castleberry® BBQ pork, or other brand
1 (10 oz) can Castleberry® BBQ beef
1 (12.5 oz) small can chicken
Small onion, chopped
Favorite BBQ sauce
Lima beans or green beans (optional)

Combine all ingredients in deep saucepan. Heat over medium heat until onion is cooked. Add sauce to desired taste.

Mandarin Orange Salad

LAURA SEABOLT

Topping
¼ C slivered almonds
1 Tbsp sugar
Dressing
1½ tsp salt
1 Tbsp parsley
2 Tbsp wine vinegar
1 dash pepper
2 Tbsp sugar
1 dash Tabasco
¼ C salad oil

Salad
2 bunches butter crunch lettuce or Romaine
1 C celery
3 green onions, chopped fine
1 (11 oz) can Mandarin oranges, drained

Caramelize almonds by mixing with sugar and stirring constantly over low heat until lightly browned. Cool on waxed paper and break into small pieces. Set aside. Combine dressing ingredients and mix well. Refrigerate for a few hours to marry flavors. Just before serving, tear lettuce into bite-sized pieces and combine with celery, onion, and oranges. Toss with dressing and nuts. Place in serving bowl. For a more decorative look, place on a larger piece of butter crunch lettuce to cradle the salad.

My family loves this salad and the little extra kick the Tabasco adds.

My Favorite Chicken and White Bean Salad

PAT CZOSNYKA

1 full rotisserie chicken, shredded
¾ C extra-virgin olive oil
3 cloves garlic, peeled and smashed
1 (3-6-inch) sprig of fresh rosemary or dried
3 anchovy fillets, coarsely chopped
¾ tsp kosher salt
¼ tsp freshly ground black pepper
Juice of one large lemon (or 2 small) and all the zest
⅓ C freshly grated Parmesan cheese
1 tsp dried oregano
½ C imported black olives, cut into fourths (pitted Kalamata recommended)
2 Tbsp tiny capers, drained
2 containers grape tomatoes
½ lb thin green beans or sugar snap peas, lightly cooked and cut into halves
2 bunches parsley or cilantro leaves, coarsely chopped
2 (15 oz) cans of white beans, drained and rinsed
Romaine or mixed green lettuce for serving or pita breads for stuffing

Place the garlic and rosemary in olive oil in a small saucepan. Heat on medium until the rosemary begins to sizzle. Remove the pan from the heat and let sit for 20 minutes, allowing the rosemary and garlic to infuse in the oil. Remove the rosemary sprig from the oil and discard. Add the garlic, anchovies, Parmesan cheese, salt, pepper, oregano, lemon zest, and lemon juice to a food processor. Process until smooth. Remove the skin from the chicken and shred the meat pieces. Place in a bowl. Combine with the dressing and let stand for 60 minutes. Toss the chicken with the olives, capers, tomatoes, parsley, canned white beans, and green beans. Season with salt and pepper. Arrange the salad on lettuce leaves on a decorative platter or place on bread to make a sandwich. It's nice stuffed in a pita too, or on a bun with a slice of red onion. ◎

BREADS

Sweet Potato Carrot Muffins (Gluten-Free)

MEAGHAN SHAFFER
whatisarutabaga.com

½ C butter
1 Tbsp fresh ginger, diced
½ C roasted sweet potato
½ C carrots, shredded and diced
2 C almond flour
½ C coconut sugar
1 tsp vanilla
1 tsp baking powder
¼ tsp salt
1 egg

Preheat oven to 425°F. Pierce a sweet potato and bake until very soft, 45-60 minutes. Melt butter over medium heat; add the ginger. Allow the butter to brown, about 15 minutes. Small brown flakes will emerge after 10-12 minutes. Once this occurs full browning will happen very quickly. Place the butter in a bowl and place it in the refrigerator. Place the carrots in the former butter pan and cook on low until soft. Once the sweet potato is cooked, reduce oven temperature to 375°F. Use an electric mixer to combine the butter in a bowl with the sugar and the egg. Add the carrots, sweet potato, and vanilla to the bowl and continue to mix well. Add the almond flour, baking soda, and salt. Mix until just fully incorporated. Place in a lined muffin pan and bake at 375°F for 25-30 minutes.

Monkey Bread

CAITLIN DENEAU

24 oz frozen bread dough rolls
3½ oz package cook-type butterscotch pudding
½ C melted butter
¾ C brown sugar
¾ tsp cinnamon
½-¾ C chopped pecans (optional)

Grease bundt pan. Place optional nuts in bottom of pan. Place rolls evenly around the pan. Sprinkle with pudding, brown sugar, and cinnamon. Pour melted butter over mixture and cover overnight. In morning, preheat oven to 350°F and bake 25-30 minutes. Let stand for a couple of minutes and invert onto platter.

Chocolate Chip Banana Bread

CAITLIN DENEAU

¾ C sugar
1½ C mashed bananas
¾ C oil
2 eggs
2 C flour
1 tsp baking soda
2 tsp vanilla
½ tsp baking powder
½ tsp salt
1 bag of mini semi-sweet mini morsel chips

Preheat oven to 350°F. Grease a loaf pan. Mix sugar, bananas, oil, and eggs in a large bowl. Stir in remaining ingredients. Pour into pan. Bake until wooden pick inserted in center or bread comes out clean, 60-70 minutes. Let cool 10 minutes, then loosen sides of pan and remove. Cool completely before slicing.

Chocolate Coffee Muffins

TAMARA STONE

½ C unsalted butter, softened
½ C brown sugar
½ C white sugar
3 Tbsp instant coffee
2 tsp vanilla extract
2 eggs
⅔ C milk
1¾ C flour
½ tsp salt
1 Tbsp baking powder
¾ C semi-sweet chocolate chips
1½ C chopped walnuts
12 (3-inch) muffin pan liners

Preheat oven to 350°F. Beat eggs and milk. Combine flour, salt, baking powder, butter, sugars, coffee, and vanilla. Add all ingredients together. Add chocolate chips and walnuts. Place muffin liners in muffin pan and fill with batter ⅔ full. Bake 20-25 minutes. Cool 5 minutes and remove.

Pumpkin Bread

ANDREA CALISE

1 (15 oz) can pumpkin puree
4 eggs
1 C vegetable oil
⅔ C water
3 C white sugar
3½ C flour
2 tsp baking soda
1½ tsp salt
1 tsp cinnamon
1 tsp nutmeg
½ tsp cloves
¼ tsp ginger

Preheat oven to 350°F. Grease and flour 3 7x3 loaf pans. Mix together the pumpkin, eggs, oil, water, and sugar. In a separate bowl, whisk together flour, baking soda, salt, cinnamon, nutmeg, cloves, and ginger. Stir the dry ingredients into the pumpkin mixture. Pour into the loaf pans. Bake approximately 60 minutes.

Sweet Potato Biscuits

AIMEE DEARSLEY

4 C all-purpose flour
2 Tbsp baking powder
2 tsp salt
1 C cold butter or margarine, cut into pieces
1 C cooked mashed sweet potato
¾–1 C buttermilk

Preheat oven to 425°F. Combine first 3 ingredients. Cut in butter with a pastry blender until crumbly. Stir together sweet potato and buttermilk; add to dry ingredients, stirring just until moistened. Turn dough out onto a floured surface; knead 3-4 times. Pat or roll dough to ½-inch thickness; cut with a 3-inch round cutter, and place on a lightly greased baking sheet. Bake 10-15 minutes or until golden.

Strawberry Nut Bread

KAREN S. FREEBERSYSER

1 C butter or margarine
1½ C sugar
1 tsp vanilla
¼ tsp lemon extract
4 eggs
3 C flour
1 tsp salt
1 tsp cream of tartar
½ tsp baking soda
1 C strawberry jam
½ C dairy sour cream
1 C chopped walnuts

Preheat oven to 350°F. Using medium speed on mixer, cream butter, sugar, vanilla, and lemon extract until fluffy. Add eggs, one at a time, beating well. Sift together dry ingredients. Combine jam and sour cream. Add dry ingredients alternating with jam mixture to creamed mixture. Beat until well-blended. Stir in nuts. Place in two 9x5x3 greased and floured loaf pans. Bake 65-70 minutes. Cool 10 minutes in pans. Remove and cool completely on racks. Makes 2 loaves. ⊚

Pumpkin Chocolate Chip Muffins

BRIAN DENEAU

3 C flour
1 C sugar
1 Tbsp baking powder
1 tsp salt
1 tsp cinnamon
2 eggs
1¼ C pumpkin
1¾ C milk
½ C butter, melted
1½ C semi-sweet mini chocolate chips

Preheat oven to 400°F. Grease or paper 24 muffin cups. Combine dry ingredients in bowl. Beat eggs, add pumpkin, milk, and butter. Stir in chips. Add dry ingredients until moistened. Spoon batter into muffin cups. Bake 20-25 minutes. Cool 5 minutes and remove from pan. ⊚

Weight Watchers Pumpkin Muffins

LISA CAMPBELL

1 box spice cake mix
15 oz can of pumpkin
1 C water

Preheat oven to 350°F. Combine all ingredients and pour into prepared muffin cups. Fill about ⅔ full. Bake according to box directions. Cool on wire rack.

Cornbread

SARAH DENEAU

1 C butter, room temperature
¾ C sugar
4 eggs
1 (15½ oz) can creamed corn
½ C shredded Monterey Jack cheese
1 C flour
1 C cornmeal
2 Tbsp baking powder
1 tsp salt

Preheat oven to 350°F. Grease 9x13 pan. Cream butter, sugar, and eggs. Add remaining ingredients and pour into pan. Bake until golden brown, about 25-30 minutes.

Sherry's Popovers

SHERRY DENEAU

3 large eggs
1 C milk
2 Tbsp butter, melted
1 tsp salt
1 C sifted flour

Preheat oven to 375°F. Beat eggs in mixing bowl until foamy. Blend in milk, butter, and salt. Add flour gradually. Beat with electric mixer until smooth. Fill heavily greased muffin pan to within ¼-inch of top (can also use a popover pan). Bake 50-60 minutes, until golden brown. Turn off heat, prick popover with a sharp knife. Leave in oven for 10 minutes to dry out.

Hot Rolls

KAREN S. FREEBERSYSER

1 package active dry yeast
½ C warm water
2½ C buttermilk biscuit mix
1 egg, slightly beaten

Soften yeast in warm water. Add remaining ingredients and beat well. Place on a lightly floured board. Knead 5-10 minutes. Roll into a rectangle ½-inch thick. Cut with a 2½-inch biscuit cutter. Place on a greased cookie sheet, cover, and let rise about 60 minutes. Preheat oven to 400°F. Bake 15 minutes. 🌀

Blueberry Muffins

AIMEE DEARSLEY

Topping
¼ C light brown sugar, firmly packed
1 Tbsp all-purpose flour
3 Tbsp chopped pecans
1 Tbsp salted butter, melted

In a small bowl, combine the brown sugar, 1 Tbsp flour, and the pecans. Stir very well. Then stir in the melted butter. Mix well. Set aside. Place topping on the muffins right before placing them in oven.

Muffins
1 C all-purpose flour
1 C whole-wheat flour
¼ C granulated sugar
¾ tsp baking powder
¾ tsp baking soda
½ tsp ground cinnamon
¼ tsp ground allspice
1 large egg
1¼ C buttermilk
1½ Tbsp vegetable oil
1 C fresh blueberries

Preheat oven to 375°F. Lightly spray muffin pan with olive oil cooking spray. In a big bowl, combine 1 C flour, whole-wheat flour, granulated sugar, baking powder, baking soda, cinnamon, and allspice. Stir it up, and make a well in the center. In another bowl, stir together the egg, buttermilk and vegetable oil. Pour this mixture into well. Stir it all together until moistened. Fold in the blueberries. Place about ⅓ C into each muffin cup. Sprinkle some of the topping on each. Bake 15-20 minutes. Muffins should be lightly browned. Cool and enjoy! 🌀

Banana Nut Bread

SUSAN LUSCOMB

1 C mashed very ripe bananas
½ C sugar
½ C plain fat-free yogurt or vanilla yogurt
¼ C margarine or butter, melted
1 tsp vanilla
1 large egg
1 large egg white
2 C all-purpose flour
1 tsp baking powder
½ tsp baking soda
¼ tsp salt
¼ C chopped pecans
1 tsp of cinnamon or nutmeg (optional)

Preheat oven to 350°F. Combine first 7 ingredients in a large bowl; beat at medium speed with mixer until well-blended. In another bowl, mix together flour, baking powder, baking soda, salt and pecans. Add flour mixture to the banana mixture mix by hand until moist. Spoon batter into 8x4 loaf pan coated with non-stick cooking spray. Bake approximately 65 minutes. Use a cake tester and insert into middle of loaf for when it comes out clean. Baking time may vary slightly depending on oven temperatures. Begin testing with the cake tester at 50-55 minutes. Cool in pan for 10 minutes, then remove and let cool completely on wire rack. For muffins: eliminate the 1 large egg white. Makes 12 muffins.

Breakaway Vegetable Bread

AVIS AYERS

3 (10 oz) cans refrigerated buttermilk biscuits
½ C margarine, melted
½ lb bacon, fried and crumbled
½ C Parmesan cheese
1 small onion, finely chopped
1 small green pepper, finely chopped

Preheat oven to 350°F. Cut biscuits into quarters, dip each piece in butter. Layer ⅓ in a lightly greased 10-inch bundt pan. Sprinkle with half of the bacon, Parmesan cheese, onion, and green pepper. Repeat layers until all ingredients are used, ending with biscuits. Bake 40-45 minutes or until done.

Blueberry Meyer Lemon Bread

PAT CZOSNYKA

1½ C all-purpose flour
1 tsp baking powder
¼ tsp salt
6 Tbsp unsalted butter, room temperature
1 C sugar
2 large eggs
2 tsp Meyer lemon peel, grated
½ C milk
1½ C fresh blueberries
Lemon syrup
4 Tbsp fresh-squeezed Meyer lemon juice
⅓ C sugar

Preheat oven to 325°F. Butter a 9.5x4x2.5-inch loaf pan. Combine flour, baking powder and salt in a small bowl. Using an electric mixer, cream butter with 1 C sugar until mixture is light and fluffy. Add eggs one at a time, beating well after each addition. Add lemon peel. Mix in dry ingredients, alternating with milk. Gently fold in blueberries. Spoon batter into prepared pan. Bake until golden brown and wooden pick inserted into center comes out clean, about 75 minutes. Meanwhile, make the Meyer lemon syrup by combining the lemon juice and sugar in a small saucepan, bring to a boil and stir until the sugar dissolves. Remove bread from oven and pierce top of hot loaf several times with a wooden pick. Pour hot lemon syrup over loaf in pan. Cool 30 minutes in a pan on a wire rack. Turn bread out of pan and cool completely on wire rack. 🌀

Zucchini Bread

NAN BENNETT AND JAN BALVEN

1¾ C sugar
1 C oil
3 eggs
1 Tbsp vanilla
1 tsp salt
3 C flour
1 tsp baking soda
¼ tsp baking powder
1 Tbsp cinnamon
2 C grated zucchini squash, leave skin on
1 C chopped pecan or walnuts

Preheat oven to 350°F. Grease 2 standard loaf pans. Combine sugar, oil, eggs and vanilla. Beat until well-blended. Combine flour, salt, baking soda, baking powder, and cinnamon. Beat into liquid mixture. Fold in zucchini and nuts. Equally distribute mixture into pan. Bake 45-60 minutes. Let cool in pans. Remove and cool completely on wire rack. Sprinkle with powdered sugar if desired. 🌀

SiDe DiSHeS

Zucchini Parmesan Crisps

MOLLY MOHRMAN

1 lb zucchini or squash
¼ C shredded Parmesan, heaping
¼ C panko crumbs, heaping
1 Tbsp olive oil
¼ tsp kosher salt
Ground pepper to taste

Preheat oven to 400°F. Slice zucchini or squash into ¼-inch thick rounds. Toss rounds with oil, coating well. Slice zucchini into ¼-inch slices. Toss in oil. In bowl combine crumbs, Parmesan, salt, and pepper. Place slices in mixture, coating on both sides. Place rounds on baking sheet. Sprinkle with remaining crumbs. Bake 23-27 minutes or until golden brown.

Dill Pickles

TERRI CHADWELL

14 C water
Cucumbers
Dill
Garlic
Hot peppers
¾ C kosher salt
1 C white vinegar
¼ tsp alum*
Canning jars
*found at grocery store with the spices

In one pan, combine ¾ C kosher salt with 1 C white vinegar and 14 C water. Bring to a boil. In another pan, boil the lids to canning jars. In the jar, place some dill, a chunk of garlic and a hot pepper or more to taste. Cut up cucumbers and fill jar. Sprinkle ¼ tsp of alum in each jar. Pour hot vinegar and salt mixture in the jar and fill to the top. Place the hot lid on the top and close jar tight. Allow to sit for 6 weeks.

Be careful, some of the jars might spill over a little, so make sure you place something under them.

Crock-pot Taters

TINA STETSON

1 (32 oz) bag Ore-Ida® southern style frozen hash browns
1 (2 lb. box) box Velveeta® cheese
2 cans cream of chicken soup
½ C sour cream
1 small onion, minced

Spray non-stick cooking spray into crock-pot or use a liner. Cut entire block of Velveeta cheese into cubes. Combine with all other ingredients in crock-pot. Cook on low for 3-4 hours, stirring occasionally.

Christy's Baked Beans

CHRISTY DENEAU

15 oz can pork and beans, drained
15 oz can great northern beans, drained
15 oz can red kidney beans, drained
8 slices bacon, cooked crisp and crumbled
1 small onion, diced
1 C catsup
½ C brown sugar
1 clove of garlic or more to taste
1 tsp prepared yellow mustard
1 tsp Worcestershire sauce
1 tsp hot sauce

Preheat oven to 350°F. Combine all ingredients in a casserole dish. Bake 45 minutes until bubbly.

This recipe is easily doubled or tripled based on your needs.

Stewed Tomatoes

JIM "THE PAINTER" GLORE

1 Tbsp cornstarch
¼ C water
14.5 oz can of stewed tomatoes
Chopped onion to taste
Chopped green pepper to taste

Combine cornstarch and water and stir well. Place in heavy saucepan and add can of tomatoes, onions, and green peppers. Simmer over medium heat for 60 minutes.

Corn Casserole

EVE HARDIN

1 (15 oz) can whole kernel corn, drained
1 (15 oz) can cream style corn
1 C sour cream
1 box Jiffy® corn muffin mix
1 C butter, melted
2 eggs, beaten
1 Tbsp sugar

Mix all ingredients and pour in 9x13 pan sprayed with non-stick cooking spray. Bake at 350°F for 45 minutes. Can be frozen. Should be lightly browned. Enjoy. ◉

Zucchini Dip and French-Fried Zucchini Sticks

KAREN S. FREEBERSYSER

Dip
¼ C mayonnaise
1 tsp horseradish
2 tsp catsup

Mix mayonnaise, horseradish, and catsup together in a small bowl. Serve in a small bowl with hot Zucchini Sticks.

Zucchini Sticks
1 large or 2 small whole zucchini
½ C milk
¼ C flour
½ tsp seasoned salt without MSG
2 C vegetable oil for deep frying

Wash and trim ends from zucchini. Quarter zucchini lengthwise. Cut quartered zucchini into 3-inch long pieces. Dip zucchini in milk to cover completely. Combine flour and seasoned salt, mix well. Take zucchini from milk and dip into flour mixture to cover completely. Heat oil to 375°F. Deep fry zucchini 2-3 minutes or until light brown. Remove from oil and drain on paper towel. ◉

Roasted Brussel Sprouts

JENNIFER OFFT

1 lb fresh brussel sprouts
¼ C olive oil
¼ tsp cayenne pepper
Salt and pepper to taste
Balsamic vinegar

Preheat oven to 400°F. Prepare sprouts by cutting off the bottom stem and cutting them in half lengthwise. Place cut sprouts into a large zip-top bag. Add all other ingredients, except for the balsamic vinegar, to the bag with the brussel sprouts, including a pinch of salt and pepper. Toss bag to evenly coat all of the sprouts. Pour contents of bag onto a baking sheet and place on the center rack of oven. Small individual leaves will be present from cutting the sprouts in half. Keep them on the tray because they get super crunchy and delicious! After 20 minutes, turn each sprout over and continue cooking for another 20 minutes. After 40 minutes of cooking time the edges of the sprouts should be dark brown and crunchy. Take the baking sheet out of oven and drizzle with balsamic vinegar while they're still hot.

This is my favorite recipe for brussel sprouts and all of my friends and family love them! ◎

Vegetable Bake

NAN BENNETT AND JAN BALVEN

¼ C butter
13¼ oz can mushroom pieces, drained
1 onion, diced
10¾ oz cream of mushroom soup
10¾ oz cream of chicken soup
15 oz can cut green beans, drained
15 oz can yellow wax beans, drained
15 oz can sliced carrots, drained
8 oz shredded cheddar cheese
8 oz shredded mozzarella cheese

Preheat oven to 350°F. In a frying pan, sauté mushrooms and onion in butter until tender. Add soups, bean, and carrots. Remove from heat and spread into 9x13 baking dish. Combine cheeses and sprinkle on top. Bake about 30 minutes until bubbly. ◎

Vidalia Onion Pie

NANCY WELLER

5 medium onions, sliced thinly
½ C butter
¾-1 C Parmesan cheese
1 sleeve (36) Ritz® crackers, crushed
2-3 Tbsp milk, added for moisture if needed

Preheat oven to 325°F. Sauté onions in butter until limp, but not brown. Place half of onions in a casserole. Sprinkle with half of cheese and half of crackers. Repeat layers. Bake uncovered, 20 minutes until light brown.

Grilled and Stuffed Portabella Mushrooms with Gorgonzola

NANCY WELLER

2 Tbsp olive oil + ¼ C
12 oz turkey sausage, casings removed
2 cloves garlic, minced
½ C mascarpone cheese, at room temperature
2 Tbsp freshly chopped thyme leaves
2 Tbsp fresh chopped oregano leaves
¾ C plain bread crumbs
1 C Gorgonzola
½ tsp kosher salt + extra for seasoning
½ tsp freshly ground black pepper + extra for seasoning
6 large Portabella mushrooms, stems removed

Place a grill pan over medium-high heat or preheat a gas or charcoal grill. In a large skillet, heat 2 Tbsp of oil. Add the turkey sausage and cook, stirring frequently, until cooked through, about 5 minutes. Add the garlic and cook for 1 minute. Remove the pan from the heat. Stir in the mascarpone cheese. Add the thyme, oregano, bread crumbs, ½ C gorgonzola, ½ tsp salt, and ½ tsp pepper. Stir until all ingredients are combined. Brush the mushrooms on both sides with remaining oil and season with salt and pepper. Grill mushrooms, stem side down, for 3 minutes. Turn the mushrooms over and grill for 2 minutes until tender. Fill each mushroom with the sausage mixture and top with the remaining Gorgonzola. Return the mushrooms to the grill and cook until the stuffing is warmed through and the Gorgonzola starts to melt, 5-7 minutes. The assembled mushrooms can also be placed on a baking sheet and cooked under a preheated broiler until warmed through.

Baked Green Beans

SARAH DENEAU

3 (14.5 oz) cans whole green beans, drained
½ C butter
½ C brown sugar
1 tsp garlic powder
1 tsp salt
1 tsp pepper

Preheat oven to 350°F. Place all ingredients in a 9x13 pan. Bake 60 minutes.

Happy Heifer Stuffed Portabella Mushroom

ERIN HEIL

2 Portabella mushrooms, washed, gills removed, stems reserved
3 garlic cloves, chopped
¼ C chopped sweet onion
¼ tsp salt
¼ tsp pepper
¼ tsp garlic powder
¼ tsp thyme
½ C chopped tomato
¼ C Italian bread crumbs
½ round of smoked Gouda cheese
2 Tbsp olive oil (twice around the pan) + more for brushing mushroom caps

Preheat oven 350°F. Heat oil over medium-high heat. Add garlic and onion and cook until soft. Reduce heat and add salt, pepper, garlic powder, thyme, tomatoes, and chopped reserved mushroom stems. Cook until some liquid has evaporated, about 4 minutes. Remove from heat and add bread crumbs until mixture has reached desired consistency. Allow to cool. Brush inside and outside of mushrooms with reserved olive oil. Add stuffing mixture to mushroom caps until full. Cook stuffed mushrooms for 15 minutes in preheated oven. Remove from oven and add smoked Gouda to the tops of stuffed mushroom caps. Cook an additional 10 minutes or until cheese is melted. Serve warm.

Potato Puffs

AVIS AYERS

½ C sifted flour
1½ tsp baking powder
Dash of salt and pepper
1 C mashed potatoes
2 eggs, well beaten

Sift flour once, measure then add to baking powder, salt and pepper; sift again. Combine potatoes and eggs. Add flour mixture. Drop by teaspoonful into hot oil. Fry until golden brown.

Grilled Mixed Vegetables

ELAINE SMITH

3 red bell peppers, seeded and halved
3 yellow squash (1 lb total), sliced lengthwise into ½-inch thick rectangles
3 zucchini (12 oz total), sliced lengthwise into ½-inch thick rectangles
3 Japanese eggplant (12 oz total), sliced lengthwise into ½-inch thick rectangles
12 cremini mushrooms
1 (1 lb) bunch asparagus, trimmed
12 green onions, roots cut off
¼ C + 2 Tbsp olive oil
Salt and freshly ground black pepper
3 Tbsp balsamic vinegar
2 garlic cloves, minced
1 tsp chopped fresh Italian parsley leaves
1 tsp chopped fresh basil leaves
½ tsp finely chopped fresh rosemary leaves

Place a grill pan over medium-high heat or heat the grill to medium-high heat. Brush the vegetables with ¼ C oil to coat lightly. Sprinkle the vegetables with salt and pepper. Working in batches, grill the vegetables until tender and lightly charred all over, 8-10 minutes for bell peppers; 7 minutes for yellow squash, zucchini, eggplant, and mushrooms; 4 minutes for asparagus and green onions. Arrange the vegetables on a platter. For great grill marks, do not shift vegetables too frequently once they've been placed on the hot grill.

Meanwhile, whisk the remaining 2 Tbsp of oil, balsamic vinegar, garlic, parsley, basil, and rosemary in a small bowl to blend. Salt and pepper to taste. Drizzle the herb mixture over the vegetables. Serve the vegetables warm or at room temperature.

Cheese Grits

MARY WHITEAKER

1 C grits
4 C water
1 roll garlic cheese
½ C butter
2 egg yolks
Salt and pepper to taste
2 egg whites, beaten

Preheat oven to 350°F. Bring water to a rolling boil with a little salt, if desired. Gradually stir in grits with fork. Cook, stirring constantly, until all water is absorbed. Stir in garlic cheese, butter, egg yolks, salt, and pepper. Stir in the beaten egg whites. Place into a greased 2-quart round casserole. Bake 45 minutes. ⊚

Sweet Potato Fluff

SANDY BOURNE

1½ C mashed, cooked sweet potatoes
2 eggs, beaten
½ C sugar
¼ C milk
3 Tbsp butter, melted
¼ tsp vanilla

Preheat oven to 350°F. Mix all potato ingredients and pour into a 10-inch casserole dish. Mix topping ingredients and spread over potatoes. Bake 30 minutes.

Topping
½ C coconut
½ C chopped nuts
½ C brown sugar
3 Tbsp melted butter
3 Tbsp flour

Mix and spread over potatoes. ⊚

Barbecued Green Beans

AVIS AYERS

3 (14.5 oz) cans French-style green beans, drained
6 strips bacon, fried, drained, and crumbled
1 C chopped onion, sautéed in bacon grease
1 C catsup
1 C brown sugar

Preheat oven to 325°F. Stir together green beans, bacon, and onion. Mix 1 C catsup and 1 C brown sugar and mix with bean mixture. Bake 2 hours. ◉

Roasted Garlic Cauliflower

PAT CZOSNYKA

6 cloves garlic, smashed
3 Tbsp olive oil
1 large head cauliflower, separated into small florets
⅓ C grated Parmesan cheese
Salt and black pepper to taste
½ C chopped fresh parsley

Preheat oven to 375°F. Infuse the oil with the garlic by putting the smashed garlic in a small pan with the olive oil. Turn heat on medium until the oil sizzles, then discard the garlic. Infusing the garlic helps to keep it from burning and turning bitter in oven. Add the spices to the olive oil and pour this mixture over the cauliflower florets in a large mixing bowl, mixing until all is well covered. Place the oiled and spiced cauliflower in a foil-lined pan that has shallow sides, like a pizza pan or shallow-sided cookie sheet. Bake 10 minutes. Remove the cauliflower from the pan. Place it back into large bowl and pour the chopped parsley all over, mixing again to be sure that the parsley is evenly distributed. Place it all back on the prepared baking sheet and pop it back into oven. After 5 minutes, sprinkle the cauliflower with Parmesan cheese and bake until the florets are soft enough to your taste and they are golden brown, about 5 more minutes. ◉

Jane Delong's Green Bean Casserole

LISA CAMPBELL

2 lbs fresh green beans, cleaned
1 tsp olive oil
3 Tbsp Parmesan cheese
1 package dry Good Seasons® Italian dressing mix

Preheat oven 350°F. Clean and trim beans, toss in oil. Toss with dressing mix. Toss with Parmesan. Place in 9x13 baking dish and bake for 30-45 minutes, stirring half-way through. ◉

Gram Renaud's Meat Dressing

DAVID RENAUD

2 medium white potatoes
2 sweet potatoes
1 lb ground chuck or sirloin
1 large yellow onion
1–2 Tbsp butter
Sage
Salt
Pepper

Peel, cube, and boil potatoes in water until soft. Dice onion finely. Melt butter in fry pan. Cook until slightly transparent. Drain, mash, and add uncooked ground chuck or sirloin. Add 1-2 C water and cooked onion. Stir, and bring to slow simmer/boil. Cook 45-60 minutes, adding water periodically so mix is consistency of a thick spread. Add sage, salt, and pepper to taste while cooking. Serve hot or cold as a side-dish, on toast for breakfast, or in other creative ways!

I am pleased to share a long-time family recipe. My grandmother (recently deceased at 99 years old) told me that she was a girl when she learned this recipe from her grandmother—so this came from my great, great grandmother! This simple side dish has always been part of Renaud Family holiday season tables. With pride, I share Gram's recipe! ◎

Mom's Strawberry Surprise

JIM "THE PAINTER" GLORE

8 oz carton of sour cream
2 large packages of strawberry jello
4 C water
6 bananas
8 oz chopped pecans
2 small containers of frozen, sliced strawberries, thawed

Mash bananas and pecans, mix together and set aside. Bring 4 C water to boil and add both jello packets. Set aside to cool. After jello has cooled down, add banana and pecan mixture along with thawed strawberries. Stir well. Pour half of the mixture into 9x13 pan. Place in freezer, do not cover. Freeze well. After jello mixture is frozen, remove from freezer, and spread carton of sour cream over entire layer. Pour remaining jello on top of sour cream and place back in the freezer. Freeze well. Remove and store in the refrigerator. ◎

DESSERT

Puppy Chow (for Humans Only)

KAREN S. FREEBERSYSER

1 box Crispix® cereal
12 oz bag of chocolate chips
½ C margarine
1 C peanut butter
1 box powdered sugar

Melt butter and chocolate chips together. Add peanut butter and stir. Pour Crispix cereal into this mixture and stir. Sprinkle with powdered sugar. Chill. Separate into small pieces. ◎

Gooey Butter Cake

NANCY HAYES

1 yellow cake mix
4 eggs, divided (2 for the crust, 2 for the topping)
½ C butter
1 lb box powdered sugar
8 oz package cream cheese

Preheat oven to 350°F. Mix cake mix with 2 eggs and butter. Pour into 13x9 pan. For the topping, mix 2 eggs, cream cheese, and powdered sugar, reserving a little powdered sugar for the top. Pour mixture on top of crust mixture. Bake 30 minutes. Sprinkle with powdered sugar and enjoy! ◎

Carrot Cake 'tween Friends

DONNA MCCALL

2 C flour
2 tsp baking powder
2 tsp baking soda
2 tsp cinnamon
1 tsp salt
3 C sugar
1½ C cooking oil or ½ C cooking oil + 1 C apple sauce
3 C grated carrots
4 eggs
1 (8 oz) small can crushed pineapple, drained
½ C chopped walnuts or any type of nuts (optional)

Combine all dry ingredients and mix. Add rest of ingredients and mix well. Pour into a 9x13 greased pan. Bake on a cookie sheet to catch any that might overflow or leave a small amount out to make a small loaf pan size bread. Bake at 300°F for 60-90 minutes, testing with a tooth pick to see if it is done. Cool completely before icing.

Icing
8 oz cream cheese
2 tsp vanilla
1 lb powdered sugar
½ C butter, softened
Dash of cinnamon

Mix all until well-blended. Double this and place most of it on the cake.

Weight Watchers®-Like Brownie Delight

MICHELLE FIENUP

1 box of low-fat brownies
1 (1-4 servings) box of sugar free white chocolate pudding
1 C fat-free skim milk
1 (20 oz) can of light cherry pie filling
2-8 oz container low-fat or sugar-free whipped topping

Make brownies as per directions on box. While the brownies are cooling, mix dry white chocolate pudding, milk, and 1 container of the whipped topping and let stand. After the brownies are cooled, begin layering ingredients in a large bowl: brownies, pudding mixture, light cherry filling, and then whipped topping. Repeat as needed. After completing layers, refrigerate overnight so that all layers can set. Substitute blueberry or raspberry filling, if preferred. 6 points per 1 C serving.

Chocolate Cream Puff Dessert

MICHELLE FIENUP

½ C margarine or butter
1 C water
1 C all-purpose flour
4 large eggs
1 (6 oz) package instant vanilla pudding
3 C milk
1 (8 oz) cream cheese, softened
1 (8 oz) whipped topping, thawed
Hershey's® chocolate syrup

Bring margarine and water to a boil. Blend flour in, beating it into a ball. Add eggs one at a time and beat well. Spread mixture into a greased 9x13-inch glass pan and bake at 400°F for 40 minutes. Cool crust.

Filling

Mix pudding, milk, and cream cheese together. Spread over cooled crust. Top with whipped topping. Drizzle chocolate syrup over the top. Keep refrigerated. Serves 12. ◎

Mounds or Almond Joy Cake

MICHELLE FIENUP

1 chocolate cake mix
24 large marshmallows
1½ C sugar, divided
1½ C milk, divided
14 oz coconut
½ C butter
12 oz chocolate chips

Preheat oven to directions on cake mix box. Bake as directed in 9x12 pan. In heavy saucepan, melt together 24 marshmallows, ½ C sugar, and 1 C milk. Remove from heat and stir in 14 oz coconut. Pour this mixture on top of warm cake and spread evenly. Let cake cool. In a saucepan, mix together ½ C milk, 1 C sugar, and ½ C butter. Bring to a boil for 3-5 minutes, stirring frequently. Remove from heat and stir in 12 oz chocolate chips. Stir until chips are melted and pour on top of cake and spread evenly.

Alternatives: For an Almond Joy cake, place almonds on top of coconut mixture before chocolate topping. ◎

Gooey Butter Cookies

TINA STETSON

½ C butter
8 oz package cream cheese
1 egg
½ tsp vanilla
1 package butter recipe yellow cake mix
Non-stick cooking spray
Powdered sugar

Cream butter, cream cheese, egg, and vanilla together in a large bowl. Add cake mix. Chill dough for 30 minutes. Turn oven to 375°F. Scoop dough by teaspoonful, roll into balls, and dip in powdered sugar. Place on a greased cookie sheet. Bake 12-14 minutes, or until tops just start to turn golden. Makes 4 dozen.

Lemon Bars

SARAH DENEAU

1 C flour
½ C butter, softened
¼ C powdered sugar
1 C sugar
2 tsp grated lemon peel
2 Tbsp lemon juice
½ tsp baking powder
¼ tsp salt
2 eggs

Preheat oven to 350°F. Mix flour, butter, and powdered sugar thoroughly in small bowl. Press evenly with hands in bottom and about ¾ up the sides of an 8x8 square pan. Bake 20 minutes. Beat remaining ingredients in a medium bowl with an electric hand mixer until light and fluffy. Pour over hot crust. Bake just until no indentation remains when touch lightly in the center, about 25 minutes. Let stand to cool, sprinkle powdered sugar on top. Cut into small squares to serve.

Salted Caramel Butter Bars

SARAH DENEAU

Crust

1 lb salted butter, room temp

1 C sugar

1½ C powdered sugar

2 Tbsp vanilla

4 C all-purpose flour

Preheat to 325°F. In a large bowl, combine the butter and sugars. Using mixer on medium speed, beat together until creamy. Add the vanilla and beat until combined. Sift the flour into the butter mixture and beat on low speed until a smooth soft dough forms. Spray 9×13 baking pan lightly with non-stick cooking spray. Press a third of the dough evenly into the pan to form a bottom crust, and place the remainder of the dough in the refrigerator to chill. Bake until firm and the edges are a pale golden brown, approximately 20 minutes. Transfer pan to a wire rack and let cool about 15 minutes. While the bottom crust is baking and the remaining dough is chilling, make the caramel filling.

Filling

1 (14 oz) bag caramel candies, *unwrapped

⅓ C milk or cream

½ tsp vanilla

1 Tbsp coarse sea salt (optional)

*about 50 individual caramels

Place unwrapped caramels in a microwave-safe bowl. Add the cream and vanilla. Microwave on high for 1 minute. Remove from the microwave and stir until smooth. If caramels are not completely melted, microwave on high for additional 30-second intervals, stirring after each interval, until smooth.

Pour the caramel filling over the crust. Sprinkle optional salt on caramel layer. Remove the remaining chilled dough from the refrigerator and crumble it evenly over the caramel. Return the pan to oven and bake until the filling is bubbly and the crumbled shortbread topping is firm and lightly golden, 25–30 minutes. Let cool before cutting into squares.

Toffee

ELLA JEAN DOLSON

1 C butter

1 C sugar

3 tsp water

3 Hershey® bars

1 C almonds + ¼ C in reserve

In heavy sauce pan, combine butter, sugar, and water. Bring to boil stirring constantly until mixture is color of light brown sugar. Quickly stir in 1 C almonds. Pour into greased 8x8 pan, top with Hershey bars. Sprinkle reserve almonds on top. Let cool and break into pieces.

Sopapilla Cheesecake Dessert Bars

EVE HARDIN

2 (8 count) packages refrigerated crescent rolls
2 (8 oz) packages cream cheese, softened
1 C + ½ C sugar
1 tsp vanilla
1 tsp cinnamon
½ C butter, melted

Spread 1 package of crescent rolls across the bottom of a 9x13 baking dish. Mix the cream cheese, 1 C sugar, and vanilla until thoroughly blended. Spread over the bottom of the dish. Top with the second package of crescent rolls, drizzle butter, then mix the remaining ½ C sugar mixed with the cinnamon. Bake at 350°F for 30 minutes. Can be served warm or cold. Enjoy! ◎

Mini Cherry Cheesecakes

KAREN S. FREEBERSYSER

16 oz cream cheese
¾ C sugar
2 eggs
1 tsp vanilla
1 Tbsp lemon juice
1 package vanilla wafers
1 (20 oz) can cherry pie filling

Mix first 5 ingredients. Use muffin papers and place one cookie in each. Add 1 Tbsp cheese mixture to each cookie. Bake in muffin pan for 15 minutes at 375°F. Let cool. Top with cherry pie filling. Makes 26-30 mini cheesecakes. ◎

Kahlua Crunch Coconut Cake

KATHRYN PARK

½ C chocolate chips
½ C pecan pieces
18.25 oz box super moist yellow cake mix
1 C Kahlua®
Slightly less than ⅔ C half-and-half
2 large eggs
½-⅔ C sweetened coconut

Preheat oven to 350°F. Coat inside of Bundt pan with cooking spray. Stir together chips and pecans and sprinkle evenly in the pan. Combine cake mix, Kahlua, half-and-half, and eggs in a large mixing bowl; beat on low for 30 seconds. Scrape sides then beat on medium for 2 minutes, scraping bowl occasionally. Stir in coconut. Pour batter into pan. Bake 40-45 minutes until toothpick comes out clean. Cool completely, then invert over a serving plate to release the cake. ◉

Cold and Crunchy

KATHY BATHE

½ C butter, melted
2½ C Rice Krispies®
1 C sweetened flaked coconut
1 C chopped pecans
¾ C brown sugar
½ gallon vanilla ice cream

In a large bowl mix together Rice Krispies, coconut, and pecans. Add melted butter and mix until well coated. Spread mixture on a roomy cookie sheet with sides. Bake at 300°F for 30 minutes, stirring every 10 minutes to avoid burning. Remove from oven place toasted mixture in bowl and immediately add brown sugar. Mix well. Let cool. Coat 9x13 pan with butter or non-stick cooking spray. Place half of toasted mixture on bottom and spread end to end. Slice ice cream and place evenly over this mixture. It will be easy to spread around. Then pour and spread remaining mixture on top. Freeze for several hours until hard. Serve immediately after removing from freezer. ◉

Gooey Butter Cake

KATHY MICELLI

1 package Duncan Hines® golden butter yellow cake mix
1 egg
½ C butter, melted
2 eggs
8 oz cream cheese, softened
3½ C powdered sugar

Preheat oven to 350°F. For the bottom layer, combine cake mix, 1 egg, and melted butter. Press into buttered 9x13 pan or 2 8x8 pans. For the top layer, combine 2 eggs and cream cheese. Beat well. Add powdered sugar or one small box and pour over bottom. Bake at 350°F until golden brown but not runny in middle. Sprinkle powdered sugar on top. Delicious! ◎

Fresh Apple Cake

ARLENE LAFAIRE

Cake
1 C oil
3 eggs
2 C sugar
1 tsp vanilla
2½ C flour
1 tsp salt
1 tsp baking soda
½ tsp baking powder
1 tsp cinnamon
3 C tart apples, finely chopped
1 C chopped pecans

Blend well the oil, sugar, eggs, and vanilla. In small amounts, add the flour, salt, baking soda, baking powder, and cinnamon. Fold in apples and nuts. Bake at 350°F in ungreased glass pan, 55 minutes.

Frosting
1 C chopped pecans
1 box powdered sugar
1 (8 oz) package cream cheese
½ C butter
1 tsp vanilla

Blend cream cheese and butter, add sugar, vanilla and pecans. Blend well, add milk if necessary. ◎

Chocolate Chip Cheeseball

TINA BODKINS

1 (8 oz) package cream cheese
1 C butter, softened
¼ tsp vanilla
¾ C powdered sugar
2 Tbsp brown sugar
¾ C mini semi-sweet chocolate chips
Cocoa to coat the cheeseball
Graham crackers

With a hand mixer cream cheese, butter, and vanilla until fluffy. Blend in sugar. Stir in chocolate chips. Cover and refrigerate for 2 hours. Shape into ball. Refrigerate 60 minutes. Just before serving, roll in cocoa. Serve with graham crackers or Anna's® wafers.

Blueberry Cream Cheese Dessert

ELLA JEAN DOLSON

1 graham cracker crust, prepared for 9x13 pan
8 oz cream cheese
1 C sugar
2 envelopes whipped topping, prepared per box instructions (Dream Whip®)
1 can blueberry pie filling or other flavor
2 Tbsp flour + 2 Tbsp butter to thicken

Preheat oven to 350°F. Prepare graham cracker crust as directed on box. Place in 9x13 pan and bake 8 minutes. Let cool. Cream the cream cheese with sugar. Prepare 2 envelopes of whipped topping, per directions. Add prepared whipped topping to cream cheese mixture and cream until well mixed and peaks form. Pour onto prepared crust and chill. Take one can of pie filling and add 2 Tbsp flour and 2 Tbsp butter. Heat on stove until thickened. Let cool then add to the cream cheese layer. Chill before serving.

Heath Cookie Bars

ANGELA SCHRIEWER

Graham crackers
1 C butter
½ C brown sugar
12 oz package of milk chocolate chips
Crushed almonds or pecans

Preheat oven to 350°F. Line a 9x13 pan with separated graham crackers. Melt butter and ½ C brown sugar together. Bring to a boil and boil for 2 minutes. Pour over graham crackers. Bake 7 minutes. Sprinkle the bag of chocolate chips over mixture. They will begin to melt. Spread smooth with a knife. Sprinkle with nuts and place in the freezer for 3-4 hours. Break into pieces. Store in freezer in air-tight container. ◉

Mississippi Mud Cake

ALEXA O'DONNELL

1½ C butter
1½ C flour
2 C sugar
⅓ C cocoa
4 eggs
1 tsp vanilla
1 C chopped pecans
1⅓ C coconut
Marshmallow cream

Preheat oven to 350°F. Mix sugar and cocoa, then add butter and eggs, mix well. Add vanilla and flour. Add coconut and pecan, mix well. Bake in 9x13 greased and floured pan for 35-40 minutes. While cake is hot, spoon marshmallow cream over cake to melt.

Icing
Powdered sugar
⅓ C cream
¼ C butter
2 tsp cocoa
2 Tbsp sugar

Add ingredients together expect powdered sugar, and let come to a boil in a double boiler. Let cool then add powdered sugar until thick. Beat until creamy, spread over cool cake. ◉

Easy No-Bake Dump Cake

PEGGY ROPPOLO

Pound cake or angel food cake
3 pints fresh strawberries
½ C sugar or to taste
1–2 containers of whipped topping, thawed

Cut cake into bite-sized pieces and dump in 13x9 baking pan. Slice strawberries and toss with sugar. Dump strawberries onto cake. Gently push cake and berries together to form level surface. Dump whipped topping onto cake and spread. Cover and refrigerate.

This is a great summertime potluck dish. Since the cake is already cut up, you only need a large spoon to serve the dessert! ◉

Aunt Buddy's Fruit Rock Cookies

MARY ELLEN CHARTRAND

1 C brown sugar
½ C butter
3 eggs
3 C flour
1 tsp baking soda
2 tsp cinnamon
½ lb black walnuts
1 lb dates
¼ lb citron or candied green cherries
¼ C candied red cherries

Cream sugar and margarine, add unbeaten eggs one at a time and beat thoroughly. Sift flour, cinnamon, and baking soda, saving enough to cover cut fruit and nuts, to keep them from sticking to each other. Add flour mixture to creamed mixture, then add floured fruit and nuts. Drop by teaspoonful on greased baking sheet. Bake at 350°F, 10-12 minutes or until lightly golden. Candied pineapple may be substituted for some of the other fruits. Makes 5 dozen.

This is a very old recipe that has been rewritten many times, as most people seem to do it from memory and they seem to turn out differently each time! ◉

Moist Pudding Chip Cookies

GINNY ENDEJEAN

1 C margarine or butter, softened
¼ C granulated sugar
¾ C brown sugar, packed
1 small box instant vanilla pudding or any other flavor
2 eggs
1 tsp vanilla
2 ¼ C flour
1 tsp baking soda
12 oz package chocolate chips or any other flavor
1 C chopped walnuts (optional)

Heat oven to 375°F. Beat margarine, sugars, pudding mix, eggs, and vanilla in large bowl with electric mixer on medium speed until light and fluffy. Mix in flour and baking soda. Stir in chips and optional walnuts. Drop onto ungreased cookie sheet. Bake 10 minutes or until golden brown. Remove from cookie sheets and cool on wire racks.

Chocolate-Hazelnut Bread Pudding

PAT CZOSNYKA

Vegetable oil spray
1 (14 oz) loaf challah bread or other firm bread, cut into 1-inch cubes
½ C chocolate chips
2 C heavy cream
2 C whole milk
9 large egg yolks
1 C Nutella® spread
¾ C + 1 Tbsp granulated sugar
4 tsp vanilla extract
¾ tsp salt
2 Tbsp light brown sugar

Line slow cooker with aluminum foil collar, then line with foil sling and coat with vegetable oil spray. Adjust oven rack to middle position and heat to 225°F. Spread bread over rimmed baking sheet and bake, shaking pan occasionally, until dry and crisp, about 40 minutes. Let bread cool slightly, then transfer to very large bowl. Mix chocolate chips into dried bread; transfer to prepared slow cooker. Whisk cream, milk, egg yolks, Nutella, ¾ C granulated sugar, vanilla, and salt together in bowl, then pour mixture evenly over bread. Press gently on bread to submerge. Mix remaining Tbsp granulated sugar with brown sugar then sprinkle over top of casserole. Cover and cook until center is set, about 4 hours, on low. Cool for 30 minutes before serving.

Apple Torte

MICHELLE STREIFF

½ C butter, softened
⅓ C sugar
½ tsp vanilla extract
1 C flour
8 oz cream cheese, softened
¼ C sugar
1 egg
½ tsp vanilla extract
⅓ C sugar
1 tsp cinnamon
4 C apples, peeled and diced
⅓ C sliced almonds

Preheat oven to 450°F. Cream together ½ C butter, ⅓ C sugar, and ½ tsp vanilla. Blend in 1 C flour. Pat firmly into spring form pan. Combine cream cheese, egg, ¼ C sugar, and ½ tsp vanilla. Beat until very smooth. Pour over crust. Mix apples, ⅓ C sugar, and 1 tsp cinnamon. Spoon over cream cheese. Top with sliced almonds. Bake at 450°F for 10 minutes. Reduce heat to 400°F, bake 30 minutes longer. Cool before removing from pan. ◉

Peanut Butter Cup

CJ SCANLON

1 C graham cracker crumbs
1 C margarine
1 lb powdered sugar
1 C creamy peanut butter
12 oz bag of chocolate chips
2 Tbsp butter
Warm water

Mix graham crackers, margarine, powdered sugar, and peanut butter together and press firmly in 9x13 pan. Place in refrigerator. Melt 12 oz chocolate chips and 2 Tbsp butter and a little warm water. Pour over peanut butter mix. Chill until cool and cut into squares. ◉

Cornflake Bars

SHERRY DENEAU

½ C sugar
½ C light corn syrup
1 C peanut butter
3 C cornflakes
12 oz bag of semi-sweet chocolate chips

Mix sugar, syrup, and peanut butter in saucepan over low heat until melted. Add cornflakes and stir to coat. Place in a 9x13 pan. Top with chocolate chips and spread as they melt over the mixture. Cool and cut into bars. ⊚

Nut Goodie Bars

SHERRY DENEAU

12 oz bag of semi-sweet chocolate chips
12 oz butterscotch chips
1 C peanut butter
1 bag mini marshmallows
1 C chopped peanuts

Melt chips and peanut butter in saucepan over low heat. Cool. Add marshmallows and nuts. Place in 9x13 pan and cool. Cut into bars. ⊚

Betty's Award Winning Lemon Sponge Pie

CHERYL LINNEMAN

Juice and rind of 1 lemon
2 Tbsp butter
1 C sugar (scant)
3 Tbsp flour
3 eggs, separated
½ tsp salt
1½ C milk
Pastry for 9-inch pie

Preheat oven to 350°F. Cream butter, add sugar and egg yolks. Beat well. Add flour, salt, lemon juice, zest, and milk. Beat egg whites until stiff. Fold egg whites into other ingredients and pour into an unbaked pie shell. Bake 40-45 minutes or until knife cut into center comes out clean.

This recipe was my mom's award winning pie. It was featured in a newspaper article in 1979 and she won a steak dinner for two at a local restaurant. ⊚

Gooey Butter Brownies

MICHELLE STREIFF

2 oz squares unsweetened chocolate
⅓ C butter
1 C sugar
2 large eggs
1 tsp vanilla extract
½ C flour

Preheat oven to 350°F. In large microwave-safe bowl, combine chocolate and butter. Microwave on high for 1-2 minutes. Stir until chocolate is melted. Stir in sugar. Mix in eggs and vanilla. Stir in flour. Spread into an 8-inch square pan lined with foil and coated with non-stick cooking spray. Bake 20 minutes. Pour topping (see below) over partially baked brownie base, bake 20 minutes, or until light golden brown and center is just set. Cool completely in pan, sprinkle with powdered sugar. Lift out of pan, onto cutting board, cut into small squares, may have to spray knife with cooking spray or butter.

Gooey Butter Topping
⅔ C sugar
¼ C butter, softened
1 egg
¼ C milk or unsweetened coconut milk
¼ C light corn syrup
1 tsp vanilla extract
½ C flour
Dash salt
Powdered sugar

Ingredients should be room temperature. In large mixer bowl, beat sugar and butter with electric mixer until light and fluffy, beat in egg. Gradually beat in milk, corn syrup, and vanilla. At low speed, beat in flour and salt until well combined. ◉

Snickerdoodles

NAN BENNETT AND JAN BALVEN

1 package white cake mix
½ C butter
1 egg
2 Tbsp sugar
1 tsp ground cinnamon

Preheat oven to 350°F. Mix cake mix, butter, and egg in large bowl with spoon until dough forms. Some dry mix will remain. Shape dough into 1-inch balls. Mix sugar and cinnamon in small bowl. Roll balls in cinnamon sugar. Place balls about 2 inches apart on ungreased cookie sheet. Bake 10-12 minutes or until set. Remove from cookie sheet to cooling rack. ◉

Easy Peach Cobbler

AIMEE DEARSLEY

1¾ C sugar
½ C butter
1 C all-purpose flour mixed with 1 tsp baking powder or 1 C self-rising flour
1 C whole milk
2 C fresh peaches

Preheat oven to 350°F. Combine peaches and ¾ C sugar. Let stand 20 minutes. Separately, mix together melted butter, milk, and dry ingredients, including the rest of the sugar, and place in casserole dish. Top with peaches. Bake 45 minutes.

This is my beloved southern Grandmother's recipe, so not low-fat, but really delicious! ◎

Monster Cookies

MELANIE LEHR

1 C butter
1 C brown sugar
1C sugar
1 egg
1 tsp cream of tartar
1 C quick oats
1 C coconut
1 C cooking oil
2 tsp vanilla extract
3 C flour
1 tsp salt
1 tsp baking soda
1 C Rice Krispies®
12 oz bag of chocolate chips or 6 oz chocolate chips and 6 oz M&M's®
1 C chopped pecans (optional)

Preheat oven to 350°F. Mix ingredients in order given. Drop by teaspoonful on greased baking sheet or baking sheet covered with parchment. If using the chocolate chip/ M&M's combo, mix in the chocolate chips, do not mix in the M&M's. Press 4-6 M&M's into the surface of each spoonful of cookie dough before baking. Bake 12 minutes. ◎

Pumpkin Cake

LOU ANN RICHARDSON

1 C pumpkin
1 C salad oil
½ tsp salt
3 C sugar
½ tsp baking powder
3 eggs
1 tsp cloves
3 C flour
1 tsp cinnamon
1 tsp nutmeg
1 tsp baking soda

Preheat oven to 350°F. Mix together salad oil, sugar, eggs, and pumpkin. Sift dry ingredients together. Combine and mix well. Bake in angel food cake pan, 75 minutes. Serve with whipped topping or eat plain. Very moist.

pet treats

Please check with your veterinarian before making any homemade
treats for your pets. Some pets are sensitive to foods and may have some
allergies to certain ingredients.

Store homemade dog treats in an air-tight container, and place them in the
freezer. Allow the treat to thaw for 10-20 minutes prior to serving to your dog.
Treats can last for up to 6 months in the freezer.

Cane

Sensitive Tummy Kong Stuffing

DEANNA SANVI

1 can pumpkin
1 apple, peeled and shredded
1 tsp ground flaxseed
Juice from can of salmon (optional)
1 (8 oz) container plain, fat-free yogurt
Peanut butter*

*for plugging small holes of Kongs

Plug small hole of Kong with a small amount of peanut butter. Mix first 4 ingredients. Fill Kongs about ½-inch from the top. Freeze and serve. Fills 6-8 large Kongs or 3-4 extra-large Kongs. Can also be frozen in ice cube trays for lots of quick snacks.

Summer Kong Stuffing

DEANNA SANVI

1 (32 oz) container plain, fat-free yogurt
2 Tbsp honey
2 Tbsp peanut butter
1 mashed ripe banana or 1 jar banana baby food*
20 blueberries
Peanut butter**

*substitute any kind of baby food, mashed fruit or mashed cooked vegetables, such as peaches, apples, sweet potatoes, or carrots

**for plugging small holes of Kongs

Plug small hole of Kong with a small amount of peanut butter. Mix first 4 ingredients in blender. Fill Kongs about ½-inch from the top. Drop 3-5 blueberries into each filled Kong. Freeze and serve. Fills 6-8 large Kongs or 3-4 extra-large Kongs. Can also be frozen in ice cube trays for lots of quick snacks.

Kitty Glop (for Ailing Kitties)

DEE RAY

12 oz boiling water
1 envelope gelatin
12 oz whole evaporated milk
2 Tbsp mayonnaise
2 Tbsp plain yogurt
1 jar pureed baby food meat, not pork (optional)
Cat vitamins (optional)

To 12 oz boiling water, add 1 envelope of gelatin, 1 can whole evaporated milk, mayonnaise, and plain yogurt. Add optional pureed baby food meat and vitamins, if desired. May freeze in portions. Thaw and serve warm. Feed to kitty with an eye dropper. ◎

Noah Shepherd's "Roll Over" Dog Biscuits

DEE RAY

2 C whole-wheat flour
¾ C rolled oats
½ C powdered milk
1 egg, beaten
5 Tbsp vegetable oil
¼ C water
1 C applesauce

Preheat oven to 350°F. In a large bowl, combine all ingredients to make a thick dough. Knead on a lightly floured surface until no lumps remain. Sprinkle with flour and roll out to ¼-inch thickness. Use cookie cutters or a small drinking glass to cut out desired shapes. Place on an ungreased cookie sheet and bake until edges are lightly browned, about 22 minutes. Makes 24 biscuits.

Let your kids help make these doggie cookies. ◎

Frosty Paws 1

AVIS AYERS

One large container vanilla yogurt
One jar of banana baby food or ripe, mashed bananas
2 Tbsp honey
2 Tbsp peanut butter

Mix and freeze in 3 oz bathroom cups with a large milk bone in the middle to use as a handle or use ice cube trays to make smaller portions.

Frosty Paws 2

NANCY WELLER

1 (4 oz) container plain or vanilla yogurt
1 ripe banana
2 oz filtered water

Blend ingredients, using a food processor or blender. Freeze in ice cube trays, and transfer to freezer bags for easy storage. Molds can also be used or small Dixie cups. If using Dixie cups, fill ⅔ full, to allow for expansion. A large measuring cup makes filling trays, cups, or molds easy. Frosty Paws are great for teething puppies.

Frosty Paws 3

NANCY WELLER

1 large container plain yogurt
1 C pure pumpkin puree
⅛ tsp carob powder

Blend ingredients in food processor or blender. Freeze in ice cube trays, and transfer to freezer bags for easy storage. Molds can also be used or small Dixie cups. If using Dixie cups, fill ⅔ full, to allow for expansion. A large measuring cup makes filling trays, cups, or molds easy. Frosty Paws are great for teething puppies.

Pumpkin Dog Biscuits

NANCY WELLER

2 eggs
½ C canned pumpkin
2 Tbsp dry milk
¼ tsp sea salt
2½ C brown rice flour
1 tsp dried parsley (optional)

Preheat oven to 350°F. In large bowl, whisk together egg and pumpkin until smooth. Stir in dry milk, sea salt, and optional parsley. Add brown rice flour gradually, combining to a stiff dry dough. Turn onto a lightly floured surface. If dough is still rough, lightly knead and press to combine. Roll dough to ¼-½ inch thick. Cut shapes with cookie cutter. Place on ungreased cookie sheet. Bake 20 minutes, remove from oven, turn over, and bake an additional 20 minutes. Allow to cool.

Daisy's Doggy Cookies

DIERBERGS SCHOOL OF COOKING

1 C rolled oats
1½ C whole-wheat flour
¼ C cornmeal
2 Tbsp dried parsley flakes
½ C creamy peanut butter
2 Tbsp vegetable oil
1 egg
½ C beef broth

Preheat oven to 350°F. In work bowl of food processor fitted with steel knife blade, process oats until finely chopped. Add flour, cornmeal, and parsley; pulse to combine. Add peanut butter, oil, and egg; process until well combined. With machine running, pour broth through feed tube in slow, steady stream; process until well combined. Turn dough out onto board; divide into 2 pieces. Roll one dough piece ¼-inch thick. Use pizza cutter to cut dough into 2 x ½-inch rectangles. Place on parchment-lined baking sheets. Repeat with remaining dough. Bake until crisp, 25-30 minutes. Makes about 11 dozen cookies.

Peanut Butter Cookies for the Doggies

KELLY GIESLER

2 C whole-wheat flour
1 C skim milk
1 C peanut butter
1 Tbsp baking powder

Mix all ingredients together and knead a few times. Roll it out about 1-inch thick. Use a cookie cutter. Place shapes on a baking sheet that has been sprayed with non-stick cooking spray. Bake at 350°F for 15 minutes.

Oatmeal Biscuits

SUSAN LUSCOMB

1½ C dry oatmeal
1 C flour
1 C cornmeal
1 egg
½ C oil
½ C water
½ tsp salt

Preheat oven to 350°F. Combine dry ingredients. Add egg, oil, and water. Mix thoroughly. Roll dough onto lightly floured surface to ½-inch thickness. Cut out with cookie cutter shape. Transfer biscuits to an ungreased baking sheet. Bake 15-25 minutes for a small biscuit, 30-35 minutes for larger biscuits. Transfer and cool on a wire rack. Store in an air-tight container.

Liver Cookies

TINA ROE

1 lb liver
1½ C flour
1½ C cornmeal
1 Tbsp garlic powder
1 C water

Puree liver in blender or food processor. Add other ingredients and blend. Pour into greased 9x13 pan. Bake at 350°F for 15-20 minutes. Sprinkle top with more garlic powder. Cut into squares and serve.

Peanut Butter Biscuits

SUSAN LUSCOMB

2 C whole-wheat flour
1 C wheat germ
1 C peanut butter
1 egg
¼ C vegetable oil
½ C water
½ tsp salt

Preheat oven to 350°F. Combine flour, wheat germ, and salt in a large bowl. Mix in peanut butter, egg, oil, and water. Roll dough out onto lightly floured surface to about a ½-inch thickness. Cut out biscuits with a cookie cutter. Transfer biscuits to an ungreased baking sheet. Bake 15-25 minutes for small biscuits or 30-35 minutes for large biscuits. Transfer to a wire rack to cool. Store in an air-tight container. ◎

Three Dog Bakery Peanut Brindle

THREE DOG BAKERY

3½ C rice flour
1 tsp ground cinnamon
½ tsp baking powder
1 egg
¼ C honey
¼ C unsalted peanut butter
½ C canola oil
1 tsp pure vanilla extract
½ C unsalted peanuts, chopped

Preheat oven to 325° F. Grease a jelly roll pan with non-stick vegetable spray. Stir together rice flour, cinnamon, and baking powder in a bowl and set aside. In a large bowl, whisk together the egg, honey, peanut butter, oil, and vanilla. Add the dry ingredients to the wet ingredients, and add 1 C water. Stir to form a stiff batter. Turn the dough out on a jelly roll pan. Cover the dough with plastic wrap. With a rolling pin, roll the dough out evenly to a ¼-inch thickness. Remove the plastic wrap and sprinkle the dough with peanuts. Lightly press them into the dough. Score the dough with a knife into 2x3 rectangles.

Bake 30-40 minutes or until the edges begin to turn golden brown. Cool to room temperature in the pan before breaking apart along the score lines and serving. Store in an air-tight container for up to 1 week, or wrap well and freeze for up to 2 months. Thaw before serving. ◎

164

Dierbergs

Entertain YOUR GUESTS WITHOUT THE MESS!

Dierbergs School of Cooking Parties

- Birthday Parties for Kids or Adults
- Dinner Parties
- Scout/Club Meetings
- Showers

Unique Entertaining with a Culinary Twist!

Bogey Hills *in St. Charles* 636-669-0049	**Clarkson** *in Ellisville* 636-394-9504	**Des Peres** *in Des Peres* 314-238-0440	**Edwardsville** *in Illinois* 618-307-3818	**Southroads** *in South County* 314-849-3698	**West Oak** *in Creve Coeur* 314-432-6505

View our class schedule and register at
Dierbergs.com

Call to schedule a party. 636-812-1336 (MO) • 618-622-5353 (IL)

AIREDALE ANTICS is truly the healthy pet paradise, offering a great selection of all natural foods, treats and nutritional supplements for cats and dogs. All foods and treats are free of fillers and have no artificial colors or flavors. We also have pet suppliers for your furry friend – crates, cat litters, shampoos, bowls, and more.

Ask about our Airedale Club Card Frequent Buyer program. Open 7 days a week – call for store hours.

7316 Manchester Road in the heart of Maplewood
314.781.PETS

At **Vitality Unlimited Spa**,
your well-being is our first concern.
Stressed minds, bodies and spirits are
soothed, centered and nourished
in our warm, friendly, relaxing sanctuary.
Visit our website for a complete list and
description of our services.
www.vitalityunlimitedspa.com

Since 1993
29 West Moody Avenue, Webster Groves, MO 63119
314.968.1808

Looking for a good painter, you've found him.

AMERICAN PAINTING CO.

5024 ULENA • ST. LOUIS, MO 63116

314-832-2671

Jim Glore

40 Years Experience • Insured • Interior & Exterior

FREE ESTIMATES

Cheescake by Jim

I make two kinds, Light & Fluffy or Regular
Price is $40.00 either variety, call for more information
At least 4 days notice

314.795.7537

Amigos Cantina

Downtown Kirkwood

120 W. Jefferson
Kirkwood, MO 63122
(314) 821-0877

amigoskirkwood.com

La Cantina

Webster Groves

35 N. Gore Ave. • Webster Groves, MO 63119
(314) 968-3256 • lacantinawebster.com

"A little taste of Mexico"

Work directly with owners, Ruth & Rick
Weddings, Proms, Formal Events
Mon, Wed, Thu, Fri 9-6pm
Sat 9-2pm

314-631-2767
8700 Gravois Rd
St. Louis, Mo 63123 (Afsfton)
email: callahanstuxedo@aol.com
www.callahanstuxedo.com

Alterations by Ruth

Bridal Gowns, Bridesmaid Dresses, Gown
Cleaning & Pressing, Gown Preservation
General Alterations - pants hemmed,
skirts, jacket sleeves and more

314-631-2767

Callahan's Travel

Ruth Deelo
Travel Planner

8700 Gravois Rd
St Louis, MO 63123
314-952-6678

Honeymoon Specialist, Families & Groups
All Inclusive resorts, Cruises, Tours
callahanstravel@aol.com

Anita's Bath & Body

handcrafted in Missouri

Pure Luxury Soap
Bath Bombs
Body Butter Bars

Bath Sorbets
Sea Salt Body Polish
Massage Oil

Whipped Body Butter

Handcrafted Bath and Body Products
All Natural, No Fillers, No Additives

www.planbsoap.com

Friendliest dog patio in St. Louis Hills!!

aya sofia
Restaurant & Wine Bar

Lunch: Tues. - Fri. 11a-2p

Dinner: Tues. - Sun. 5p

Brunch: Sun. 10a-2p

Wine Wednesdays:
half price wine on select bottles

Happy Hour: Tues. - Fri. 5p-7p

Catering: Special Events & Private Parties

6671 Chippewa : : www.ayasofiacuisine.com : : 314.645.9919

Baumann's Fine Meats

8829 Manchester Road
Brentwood, MO 63144

314-968-3080

www.baumannsfinemeats.com

Delivery • Special Orders • Caterimg

Catherine Hughes

Animal Communicator

I give animals a voice.

314-616-4780
catherine@coolaideclinic.com
www.coolaideclinic.com

Canine Cookies N Cream Dog Bakery

All Natural Dog Treats & Sweets
So Come On Down And Sniff Around

822 S Main Street
St Charles, MO 63301
636-443-2266

- *Bakery Quality Dog Treats*
- *Dog Ice Cream (Made on Site)*
- *Toys and Unique Gift Items*

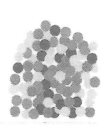

INTRODUCING

Twice as Nice Shop

314-873-0288

and

RETRO BOB'S ANTIQUES

314-560-5869

7317-7319 South Broadway • St. Louis, Mo 63111

Stray Rescue Wednesdays

10% of days profit will be donated to the Stracks Fund.
(Emergency Medical Fund)

Bid Box Thursday's

Every Thursday we will take bids
on everything in the store.

DON'T PAY RETAIL PRICES, COME SEE US!!

We have antiques, home decor, collectibles,
vintage items, retro items and appliances

Our staff will sniff out your tax refund

Bratkowski CPAs

13354 Manchester Road   St. Louis, MO   63131

314-965-8633

www.bratkowskicpas.com

Fiduciary Litigation
Estate Planning: Pet Trusts,
   Wills, Powers of Attorney
Probate & Trust Administration
Guardianship & Conservatorship

Medicaid & VA Planning
Long-Term Care Planning
Special Needs Trusts
Medicare Set-Aside Arrangements
Veteran Benefits

Stray Rescue – Doug

The Elder & Disability Advocacy Firm

of Christine A. Alsop, LLC

3703 Watson Road • St. Louis, MO 63109

314-644-3200 phone • 314-206-4745 fax

calsop@alsopelderlaw.com • www.alsopelderlaw.com

CLARK ANIMAL HOSPITAL

"We Share In Your Pet's Care"

10510 MANCHESTER ROAD
KIRKWOOD, MO 63122

314-966-2733
FAX 314-966-4699
www.clarkanimal.com

 Find us on
Facebook

Tim A. Pennington, D.V.M • Jeffrey R. Coggan, D.V.M.
Catherine A. Pennington, D.V.M. • Julie Dobslaw, D.V.M.
Allison Blake, D.V.M. • Margaret Farnon, D.V.M.

CRESTWOOD COIN & JEWELERS

Diamonds • Gold • Coins • Bridal Sets
Remounts • All Fine Swiss Watches
Flatware • Estates • Insurance Appraisals

10021 Watson Road
St. Louis, MO 63126
crestwoodcoin.com

314-821-7878

Tom Shearburn

AVON

Sales Representative
KRISTIN KLEESCHULTE

314-952-1866

IN2SPORTZ@CHARTER.NET
WWW.YOURAVON.COM/KKLEESCHULTE

Daniel's Construction

Everything from
Kitchen and Bath Remodel
to Total Rehabs

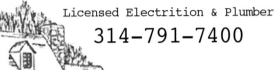

Licensed Electrition & Plumber

314-791-7400

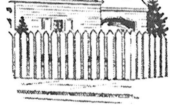

EL-MEL INC.

WHEELHORSE/SNAPPER
TORO/LAWN-BOY/ECHO
REDMAX/POULAN PRO

Lawnmower Sales & Service
Pet Food & Pet Supplies

6185 N. HWY.67
FLORISSANT, MO 63034
314-741-2117
FAX 314-741-3596

2139 FIRST CAPITOL DRIVE
ST. CHARLES, MO 63301
636-946-9049
FAX 636-946-0786

OLD ORCHARD TOWING
★
COMPLETE AUTOMOTIVE ROAD SERVICE
TOWING • WINCHING
LOCK-OUTS • TIRE CHANGES

"We treat your car with care."

28 years in business
★
JOE BLAKEMORE

314-537-4403

The Clean Machine

🐾 Window Cleaning

🐾 Pressure Cleaning

🐾 Gutter Cleaning

Call The Clean Machine for your FREE estimate

314-489-8458

Young

Painting & Decorating

Interior 🐾 Exterior

Residential 🐾 Commercial

Complete Restoration
Insured for Your Protection

For your FREE estimate call

314-489-7476

Do You Love Candles?

PARTYLITE®

FREE Shopping Sprees Available!!
Get a few friends together for a unique Girls' Night Out or
Happy Hour to experience fragrance, decorating & FUN

Or place your order 24/7 on my website at:
www.partylite.biz/ginafletcher Phone: 636.343.1033

Become a Preferred Member to earn free Candle Cash each time you shop!

Certified Plant
Based Cooking
Instructor,
Nutrition Coach,
Personal Chef

Caryn Dugan
www.STLVegGirl.com

The Most Innovative Approach
TO DOG CARE IN ST. LOUIS

OPEN
24/7
365

Happy Tails Canine Enrichment Center has a unique attitude and atmosphere designed to ensure maximum care, comfort and convenience for you and your furry family member.

A MUST SEE FOR ANY DOG OWNER!

IN ST. LOUIS, WE ARE THE FIRST IN OUR INDUSTRY TO OFFER THESE AMENITIES:

~ Totally open environment dedicated to your dog's well being

~ Open 24 hours, 7 days a week, and 365 days a year

~ 21,000 sq ft of Prostyle AstroTurf covered play yard

~ Pick up and drop off at any hour

~ 8,000 square feet of indoor playrooms

~ Online reservations

Our complete list of services make us the one-stop shop for all your dog care needs:

• Bed & Biscuit Boarding [our facility or your home]
• Stay & Play Daycare
• Full-Service Grooming
• In and Out Home Visits
• Walking and Exercise
• Pick Up and Delivery Services
• Pet Parties

~ TRAINING & AGILITY BY ~

PLAY YARDS   LOBBY   GROOMING   TRAINING   BOARDING & DAYCARE

314-291-DOGS (3647)
2920 North Lindbergh Boulevard 63074 | www.HappyTailsInc.com

Miller's Auto Repair
Since 1979

Mike Miller
President

12300 Bellefontaine Rd
Saint Louis, MO 63138
(314) 741-2534

520 Little Hills
Saint Charles, MO 63301
(636) 949-2334

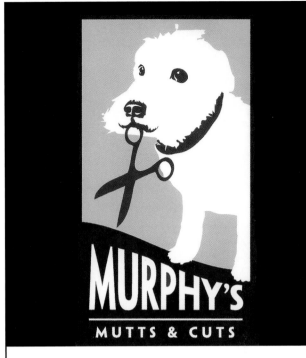

INFO @ MURPHYSMUTTS.COM
2307 CHEROKEE ST.
ST. LOUIS, MO 63118

314-771-3338

THE FENTON GANG

Nan, Jan, Holly, Neah,
Momma Cartwright,
and Raisinette

Stray Rescue – Cupid

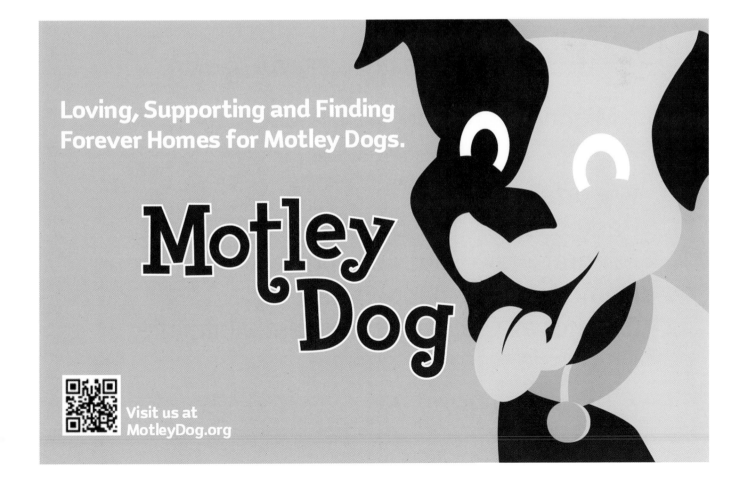

Loving, Supporting and Finding
Forever Homes for Motley Dogs.

Motley Dog

Visit us at
MotleyDog.org

Tupperware®

Your local Connection to buy or
sell Tupperware is

Barbara L Braden
Executive Director
http://My.Tupperware.com/
MightyRiverSales

(314)402-8350

MightyRiverSales@My.Tupperware.com

We offer…
* Parties for 3—100 people
* Fundraisers—Earn 40% profit for your group
* Home Business Opportunity
* Gifts for all Occasions that last a Lifetime
* No hassle warranty service

Call or click today!

OMNI HOTELS & RESORTS
majestic | st louis

You're invited to experience Mahogany Grille!

Enjoy breakfast a la carte with two different buffet options, choose lunch or dinner from our new updated menu, or just relax with a refreshing cocktail from the bar.

Hours of Operation
Daily Happy Hour: 4:00 pm - 7:00 pm
Bar Open till 11:00 pm every night

Breakfast
Mon - Fri: 6:30 am - 9:00 am
Sat - Sun: 7:00 am - 12:00 pm

Lunch
Mon - Fri: 11:00 am - 2:00 pm
Sat - Sun: No lunch served

Dinner
Sun - Sat: 4:00 pm - 10:00 pm

Mahogany Grille • 1019 Pine Street, St. Louis, MO 63101
314-436-2355 • omnihotels.com/stlouis

Self Serve Dog Wash

Using our organic spa products and grooming supplies and... we clean up the mess!

Bedding
Toys
Leashes
Collars
Bowls
All Natural Dog and Cat Food
All Natural Treats
Organic Spa Products

2414 Taylor Rd. Wildwood, MO 63040
www.oneluckymutt.com | (636) 458-8838

Hours Mon-Thur. 10am-6pm
Fri-Sat 9am-5pm Sun. Noon-4pm

Plus Size Resale & Alterations

Spray Rescue—Mirana

- Brand Names & Designer
- Consignment & Layaway
- Specializing in Sizes 12-6x
- Professional Alterations
(men's & lades alterations, any item)

Panache Plus www.panacheplusresale.com

5400 S. Kingshighway @ Eichelberger (314) 352-3838

Paramount Salon

donna o cohen
owner/stylist

tracy emerson
stylist

"The best haircut is the one that you love."

Paramount service in an intimate setting.

2173 Big Bend Blvd.   St. Louis 63117

314 644 2525

Sandra B. Kapsar, CPA

3368 A Oxford Ave
Maplewood, MO 63143
Phone (314) 226 - 9828

Fax (314) 226 - 9943
sbkapsar@sandrabkapsarcpa.com

Tax Preparation & Planning • Bookkeeping • Payroll

WAKE UP
SAINT LOUIS

REPORT ANIMAL ABUSE
314.771.6121 ext: 232

MAKE A DIFFERENCE. SAVE A LIFE.

SUGAR MAGNOLIA

Sugar Magnolia

NEED A LIFT?

No matter your band or cup, Sugar Magnolia Boutique can LIFT you up.
Professional Bra Fittings · Cup sizes AA-H and Band Sizes from 30-50

WINNER 2012 BEST ST. LOUIS

LINGERIE,
LOUNGEWEAR
& BURLESQUE

Open Tue, Wed, Fri & Sat 10AM to 5PM • Thur 10AM to 7PM • Closed Sun & Mon
38 N. Gore Ave. Webster Groves, MO 63119
www.sugar-magnolia.com 314.395.9159

cards + gifts
Relish
... a little something extra

Relish Cards + Gifts stocks unique merchandise that you can only find here! We buy from small vendors and change items regularly. From cards, to flowers, to gifts for that "hard to buy for person" .. it's all here.

CWE: 22 North Euclid Avenue • St. Louis, MO 63108 • **314-367-9333**
relishcardsandgifts.com • facebook.com/relishcardsandgifts

The Great Frame Up
WHERE PICTURE FRAMING IS AN ART.®

Warm and cozy, sleek and urban, or forever classic. No matter your preference, let our custom framing professionals help you express your style. We can find the perfect design for anyone. Our knowledgeable staff of experts is extensively trained to assist you in capturing just the right custom frame design to complement your room, your lifestyle, your budget and even your personality.

CWE: 22 North Euclid Avenue • St. Louis, MO 63108 • **314-367-9333**
South County: 4481 Lemay Ferry Rd • St. Louis, MO 63125 • **314-892-8333**
stlouis.thegreatframeup.com • facebook.com/thegreatframeupstl

S.o.S Tattoo Parlor
Tattoo & Piercing
314.962.5777

Find us on Facebook

7919 BigBend
Webster Groves MO

Wolfgang's Pet Stop

Pet Care & Services
GROOMING~DAYCARE~TRAINING
BOARDING~NUTRITION~DIY DOG WASH

1820 Washington Ave. STL, MO 63103

New Downtown Location
314-539-9653

Central West End
330 North Euclid Ave. STL, MO 63108
314-367-8088

WOLFGANGSPETSTOP.COM

Where Your Purchase Makes a Difference

Jewelry
Baskets
Coffee, Tea & Cocoa
Fine Décor & Gifts
Nativities

Plowsharing Crafts is a
nonprofit retail organization that offers a wide variety
of Fairly Traded handcrafted products
made by artisan groups in more than 40 countries.

University City   6271 Delmar   314-863-3723
Kirkwood   137 W. Jefferson Ave.   314-909-9401
Edwardsville   224 North Main St.   618-692-6919

IN MEMORY OF
KYLE TORRETTA
LOVE,
MOM AND DAD

Touched By A Canine – Therapy Dogs

Find us on Facebook

We support Stray Rescue !!
Your performance is High In Trial !!

From Tina & The Crew
Lake's Anniebelle Roe
Lake's Wannabee Herby D Luv Bug CDX, RN, CGC, TT
Lake's Wannabee Twigger Happy CD, RN, CGC, TT
UCH UCDX URO3 Kyteral's Coup de Grand Finale CDX, RAE, CGC, THD, TDI, TT, HIT

YOUR HOME BISTRO

Personal Chef Service

636-938-9933

www.yourhomebistro.com

**Personal Chef Dinner Service,
In-Home Cooking Classes,
Interactive Dinner Parties, Customized Meals**

**Let Chef Pam solve your
"What's For Dinner?" dilemma.**

*Your Home Bistro…
a delicious beginning to a relaxing evening!*

Checkered Cottage

135 W. Jefferson   Kirkwood, MO 63122
314-909-7233
www.checkeredcottage@sbcglobal.net

Paper Crafting Supplies

Classes

re-create Consignment

Gifts

Stray Rescue–Mr. Stapleton

Three Dog Bakery
THE BAKERY FOR DOGS

**The one-stop shop for everything dog.
All-natural food & treats, dog toys,
rawhides, collars and more!**

Bring your dog and visit us today.
(they will let you know what they love)

All dogs on leashes welcome

*we love dogs,
and dogs love us!*

**Three Dog Bakery®
1208 Town & Country Crossing Drive
636-527-3364
www.threedogstl.com**

A.M. Clark and Sons, Inc.

7879 Big Bend Blvd.
Webster Groves, MO 63119

314-961-7500

Locally owned and operated • *Like us on Facebook*

Jake and Josie

AZAR AUTOMOTIVE

COMPLETE AUTOMOTIVE SERVICE

1620 N and South Rd.   •   St Louis, Missouri 63130

(314) 426-2323

email: azarautomotive@mechanicnet.com • www.azarautomotive.com

Hatha Yoga
Pilates
Tibetan Singing Bowls
Insight Meditation
Pre-natal Yoga
MassageTherapists
Workshops & Retreats

bigbendyoga.com

big bend yoga center
a place to center yourself

"My favorite yoga pose? Downward Facing Dog!"
—Luna
Stray rescue

Luna in Savasana

Big Bend Yoga Center proudly supports Stray Rescue of St. Louis, but sorry, BBC yoga is only for humans.

PET PORTRAITS
BY LAUREN HEIMBAUGH

Have a favorite picture of your dog or cat? Send it to me and I will create a portrait based off of this photo with colored pencils.

Base Prices: (This includes the bust of the pet: head, neck, upper chest and collar)
8×10" color drawing starting at $250
11×14" color drawing starting at $300

Contact me at lheimbaugh@gmail.com or 636-399-0900 and see bewareoftreescreations.com for examples of my previous work.

Sophie, a stray brought to the Highland Animal Shelter. She is the second AKC ALL AMERICAN CANINE PARTNER to attain this title, and to receive an invititation to compete at the AKC National Obedience Invitational in 2012, since AKC started the partner program.
She has her UTILITY DOG EXCELLENT title.
Sophie attained her OBEDIENCE TRIAL CHAMPION title on July 7, 2013.

Lori Richardson, RN

Reiki Master
PetMassage Practitioner
Animal Reiki

Pet Massage
In-home Pet Sitting

(314) 445-9990
Jethrole1414@sbcglobal.net

HLS INC.

HUTCHISON
LANDSCAPE
SERVICES

We support Stray Rescue.

631-728-0167
WWW.HUTCHISONLANDSCAPE.COM

JUST WOODEN FENCES

"Since 1998"

- Ultimate Construction Detail
- Fair Prices
- Free Estimates

Walt Thorngren - Owner
314.773.8701

w w w . j u s t w o o d e n f e n c e s . c o m

Working long hours?
Traveling frequently?
Wanting to go on vacation?
Sharing your home with a special needs pet?
Needing a reliable back-up when friends/family/neighbors
aren't available to care for your pet(s)?

Time to call a professional pet sitter, and let us
care for your pet(s), your home and provide peace-
of-mind!

Proud
MEMBER

314-717-1PET /info@kritterkare4u.com

INSURED AND
BONDED BY:

CERTIFIED

www.kritterkare4u.com

Trusted Professionals with a Passion for Your Pets!
Metro St. Louis- east and west of the river

MICKEY

BENSON

1362 BIG BEND SQUARE
BALLWIN, MO 63021

636-225-2222

2956 DOUGHERTY FERRY
ST. LOUIS, MO 63122

636-529-1121

We love dogs & Stray Rescue

MARYGROVE
GIVING CHILDREN ROOTS TO HEAL AND GROW

2705 Mullanphy Lane
Florissant, MO 63031
314-830-6201
info@marygrovechildren.org
http://www.marygrovechildren.org/

LP Miceli Inc.

3800 Hampton
St. Louis, MO 63109

All lines independent insurance agency

Tina Miceli
314-832-6667 direct
314-802-7607 fax
tmiceli@lpmiceliinc.com

Alma

Zealand

MIXED BREED DOG CLUB
ST. LOUIS CHAPTER

MIXED BREED DOG CLUB

ST. L OUIS CHAPTER

YES there is a special club for our special MUTTS.

We meet every 4th Tuesday 7 pm

at the Corner Coffee House in Ferguson, MO

(Except August and December)

We participate in a lot of extra events

around the City and County

We also have shows twice a year

at Westinn Kennels in Wentzville, MO

MUTTS can earn all the titles that the Pure breeds do.

Including Lure Coursing, Championship breed, Rally, Obedience,
and other things.

Contact Phyllis Massa-Busch at huskyslady@ gmail.com

Training available

at January Wabash Park, Ferguson 521-4661

North County Obed. Training Club 741-2445

4401 N USHwy 67

North County offers $5 off for all dogs adopted from Stray Rescue (Proof)

MOTORCYCLES-NEW, USED & VINTAGE | SERVICE | PARTS | APPAREL
5745 DALE AVE. | **DOGTOWN** | **314.732.0357** | **WWW.MOTORRADSTL.COM**

St. Louis Muttropolitan

Pet Grooming
(all breeds of dogs and cats too)

Boarding • Doggy Daycare

5280 Fyler at Sublette

314.647.7911

info@stlmpg.com • www.stlmpg.com

Daycare Hours 6:30am - 7:00pm
(or the last dog goes home)
Monday thru Saturday

Stray Rescue – Tomfoolery

www.provalodeli.com
find us on facebook and twitter

314-962-5500

We Deliver • Catering
Locally owned and operated

Sandwiches, Wraps, Pizza, Salad and Soup

"Stop By and try our famous Pretzel Bread Sandwiches!"

BUCHHEIT COUNSELING
— HEALING THROUGH SELF —

Steven Buchheit LPC
9374 Olive Blvd.
Suite 202
St. Louis, MO 63132
314-698-3114

Stray Rescue–Laika

PAPERS WITH PERSONALITY

CLAUDIA HOFFMANN

Offering Invitations and Stationery
Weddings one of our many specialities
Custom Printing available

12095 MANCHESTER ROAD   PHONE: 314-821-6561
DES PERES, MO 63131   PAPERPATCH@GMAIL.COM

PAPERPATCHINVITESYOU.COM

FOUR DIRECTIONS
HIKING

www.fourdirectionshiking.com

PATRONS

90 DEGREES WEST

TIGER LILY

KAREN BRADBURY

HOLY CREPE FOOD TRUCK

SAMANTHA AND BOB HIGGINS

SCOTT AND MARY WHITEAKER

BRIAN, SARAH, AND CAITLIN DENEAU: PROUD STRAY RESCUE VOLUNTEERS

JAN BLOMEFIELD AND ROXIE

MARGIE AND JIM REDENBAUGH

JAMES R. & KAREN S. FREEBERSYSER

KATHY MICELI

APRIL CAYCE

NANCY SCHULZE-HOPE EVERYONE FINDS A HOME AS GOOD AS WE DID...TOBI, LEMMY, OZZIE AND ACE SCHULTZ

THE BERGFELD FAMILY

ELAINE SMITH

TINA MICELI

CHERYL LINNEMAN

SHAWNA DAVINROY

DAWN AND MIKE HARROD

MARY KAY CANDIDO

LEA WILKE AND CHRIS MOODY IN MEMORY OF BUDDY

LAUREN SEABOLT

THANK YOU RANDY AND TEAM FOR ALL YOU DO FOR OUR 4 LEGGED FUR CHILDREN. LISA PEPPER

BELLA, BRIAN AND SIMON GHIASSI

DAVID STRONG

AMY SCHUSTER

TRISH AND ERIC CARTER

AMERICAN VENDING MACHINES

THE STONE FAMILY

CAROL GREGERSON